# BRAZILIAN STYLE

© 2011 Assouline Publishing
601 West 26th Street, 18th floor
New York, NY 10001, USA
Tel.: 212-989-6810  Fax: 212-647-0005
**www.assouline.com**

ISBN: 978 1 61428 013 2
10 9 8 7 6 5 4 3 2

Color separation by Luc Alexis Chasleries
Printed in China
Design by Camille Dubois

ARMAND LIMNANDER

# BRAZILIAN STYLE

ASSOULINE

Santa Ifigênia bridge, São Paulo

# FOREWORD

The moment Armand Limnander asked me to think about what Brazilian style means to me, I remembered all the wonderful, creative people I have met throughout my acting career: musical prodigies like Caetano Veloso, Gilberto Gil, Chico Buarque, and Tom Jobim, who changed music forever; the late Roberto Burle Marx, who somehow managed to combine art with plants; Oscar Niemeyer, whose sinuous architectural lines remind me of the way girls walk on the streets of Rio, sashaying as if they always have a song playing in their heads. It occurred to me that, while these geniuses were profoundly erudite, they always rose above it all. With a joke or a smile, they made me believe that everything they knew, they had simply learned from life.

That, to me, is the essence of Brazilian style. There is an innate sense of intuition in everything we do; it's as if we are constantly looking for a deeper connection to the human soul. Whenever I look at Brazilian art, fashion, or design, I immediately have a sense of the people behind the work: men and women of all races, backgrounds, and beliefs, who nonetheless form a cohesive whole. When a foreigner arrives in Brazil, he or she is Brazilian the next day; it has always been that way, and that is reflected in the way we live.

I have always felt that Brazil is the richest country in the world, so I am thrilled to see that more and more visitors are having the chance to appreciate everything we have. When some of my friends travel to Brazil for the first time and tell me about it afterward, it's always as if they are speaking in capital letters and using exclamation points: MUSIC! FUN! DELICIOUS! This book offers a glimpse of what my country has to share with the world. I'd like for you to think of *Brazilian Style* as a trailer for the best movie you will ever see.

SONIA BRAGA

# INTRODUCTION

When I first told a few friends that I was working on a book called *Brazilian Style,* they seemed a bit perplexed. Why Brazil? It was a fair question: After all, I'm Colombian and French, and although I've traveled extensively in Brazil, I've never lived there. I'm well aware that I'm not an academic authority on Brazilian culture; I studied Portuguese in college, but what I speak is more like "Portuñol"—a weird disfiguration of my native Spanish with an "ão" at the end of almost every word. After a while I started to wonder, should I really be doing this?

A tour of several bookstores made me stop doubting myself. Everywhere I looked, there were tomes on almost everything you could possibly want to know about Italy, France, England, and the United States, but pretty much zilch on Brazil. And yet, I felt sure it was one of the most thrilling places on the planet. So I convinced myself that if no one else had thought of doing this book, it might as well be me. In all honesty, it may have been that I just needed an excuse to keep going back for more caipirinhas on the beach.

I first visited Brazil with an American friend in 2001, just before New Year's Eve. We flew from New York to Rio, arrived in Ipanema and went on an impromptu tour, bags in hand, of all the waterfront hotels until we found one we liked, and took rooms for about $100 a night. That was then, this is now: Today, pretty much the entire city is booked up for New Year's months in advance—and the same rooms we sauntered into without a reservation now go for about eight times as much.

That's just one example of the speed with which Brazil is changing. By some accounts, its economy is now the fifth largest in the world, and although it still has a long way to go in terms of vanquishing poverty, in the past decade millions of its citizens have entered a steadily growing middle class. Unlike the other rapidly developing BRIC countries (Russia, India, China), Brazil has no looming international conflicts, border disputes, or thorny political issues; in fact, the opposite is true—everyone seems to love Brazil. Now that Brazilians are hosting the FIFA World Cup in 2014 and the Olympics in 2016, Rio and São Paulo are getting extreme makeovers. Historic buildings are being renovated, parks are being replanted and expanded, and world-class architects are showing off new museums and futuristic structures. It's the country's moment to shine, its chance to prove to the world that it has come of age.

The arrival of Brazil as a serious player in the global arena means the Brazilian market is being taken very seriously indeed. Almost every luxury brand on the planet has an outpost in São Paulo; on Madison Avenue and the rue du Faubourg Saint Honoré, Brazilians rival Russians and Chinese as the new power shoppers. But Brazil's accelerated expansion isn't just about consuming: When a country becomes a superpower, it naturally tends to export its culture, and Brazil—which has been straddling the old and new worlds for as long as it has existed—has much to offer in that regard. Its combination of tradition and modernity and its unique blend of indigenous, African, and European cultures redefine what cosmopolitan means for the twenty-first century.

The aim of this book is to bring together Brazil's sensual music, exacting architecture, rich culinary tradition, carefree fashion, and cerebral artistic movements. Every country has stereotypical visual cues that define its culture; in addition to those, I was interested in more obscure references that appealed to me on a purely personal level. I selected a wide range of items that, in my mind, offer a bird's-eye view of the past, present, and future.

*Brazilian Style* is organized like an informal encyclopedia, to reflect the organic way in which my obsession grew: The more I learned about Brazil, the more I wanted to know. However, it is in no way encyclopedic. I'm sure there are plenty of important people, places, and movements that did not make the cut; sometimes I felt like I could have kept going for a thousand more pages. Perhaps this effort will inspire others to cover some of the many topics I have overlooked. In the meantime, I hope you'll enjoy perusing *Brazilian Style* as much as I did putting it together.

ARMAND LIMNANDER

# G

## GISELE

At age 14, Gisele Bündchen enrolled in a modeling course with two of her five sisters to improve her posture for an upcoming debutante ball in her home-town of Horizontina. Seventeen years later she is a goodwill ambassador for the United Nations Environment Pro-gramme and, according to *Forbes,* the best-paid model of all time.

# P

## PELÉ

In a country where football rules, Pelé is king. He won his first World Cup at age seventeen, played in three more, and became the top scorer in the history of the sport. Pelé has also appeared in several films and television series, and had a postage stamp issued in his honor.

# N
## NIEMEYER, OSCAR

Brazil's most emblematic modern architect, often referred to as a "sculptor of monuments," Oscar Niemeyer is famous for his work on the United Nations headquarters in New York, as well as many iconic buildings in Brasília, and the Museum of Contemporary Art in Niterói (pictured). Niemeyer was awarded the prestigious Pritzker Prize in 1988, at age eighty-one.

# S
## SUGARLOAF

A huge part of Rio's charm comes from its unique coastal geography, punctuated by granite and quartz monoliths that seem to sprout out of nowhere. *Pão de Açúcar,* the most famous of all, inspired a Herb Alpert song and has appeared in the James Bond film *Moonraker* as well as in an episode of *The Simpsons.*

# CARLOS, ROBERTO

Known as the king of Latin music, Roberto Carlos, who had his heyday in the 1960s and '70s, has sold over 120 million albums. In addition to Portuguese, he has recorded in Spanish, French, English, and Italian.

# O F

## O RIO DE JANEIRO

### FASHION SHOOTS

Bruce Weber's seminal 1986 book O *Rio de Janeiro* made the city a major style destination. Since then, globe-trotting photographers like Mario Testino and Michael Roberts have documented Rio's hedonistic scene.

# F

## FOOTBALL

In Brazil, you can never have too much football—or cacao. Artist
Vik Muniz paid a sweet tribute to his country's most beloved
sport with this work, part of his Pictures in Chocolate series.

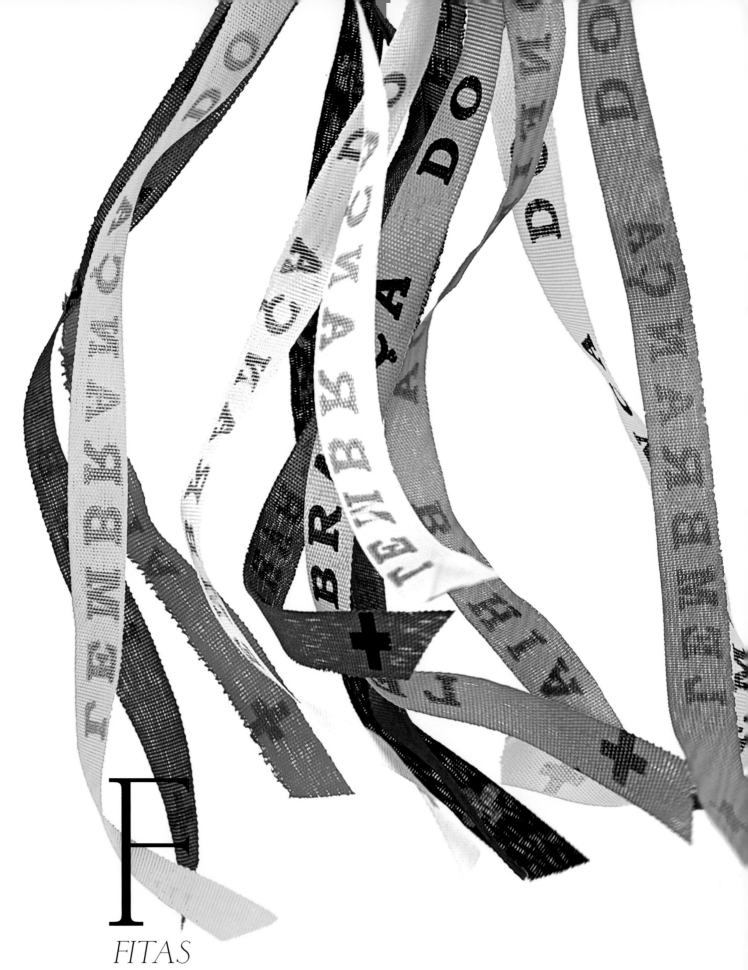

# F

## *FITAS*

Tie one on and make a wish. These colorful ribbons say "In Remembrance of the Lord of Bonfim of Bahia," alluding to the eighteenth-century Senhor do Bonfim church, where visitors still petition for miracles. The fita is tied on the wrist with three knots, and when it disintegrates and falls off—of its own accord—your three wishes come true.

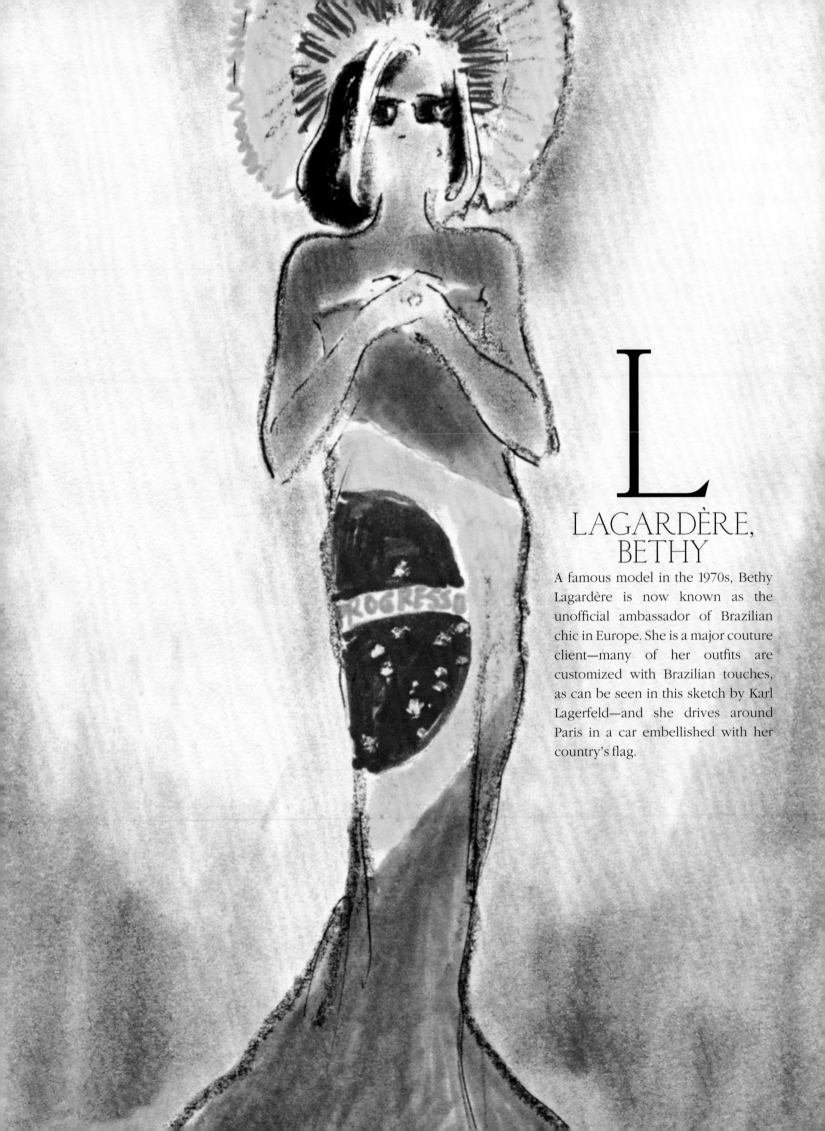

# L
## LAGARDÈRE, BETHY

A famous model in the 1970s, Bethy Lagardère is now known as the unofficial ambassador of Brazilian chic in Europe. She is a major couture client—many of her outfits are customized with Brazilian touches, as can be seen in this sketch by Karl Lagerfeld—and she drives around Paris in a car embellished with her country's flag.

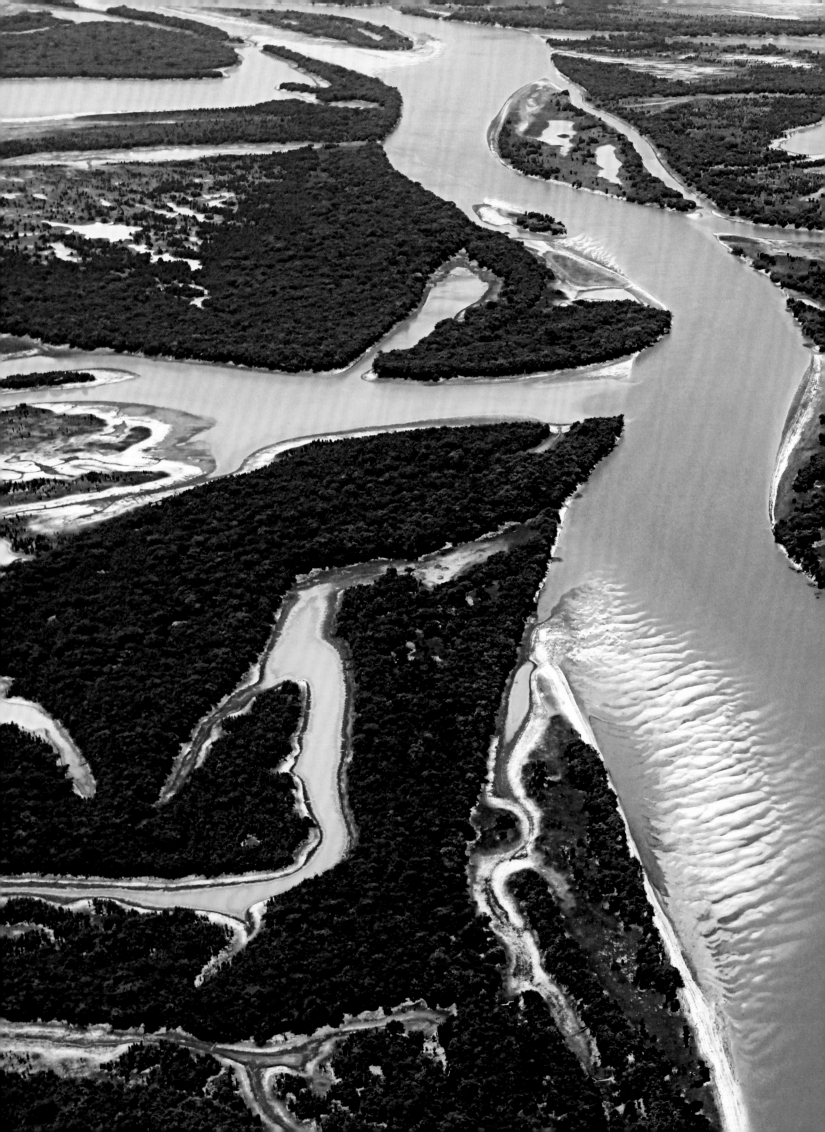

# A
## AMAZON RIVER AND RAIN FOREST

The Amazon River is the second longest in the world, and represents one fifth of the world's total river flow. Its rain forest covers about 2.5 million square miles—roughly half the total left on earth. Although it is part of nine South American countries, the vast majority is in Brazil, and despite local and international efforts to combat deforestation, the area (and its biodiversity) is shrinking at an alarming rate.

# ORFEU NEGRO

Parts of it haven't aged well, but this 1959 film, a reimagining of the classic legend of Orpheus and Eurydice set in a favela, won the Palme d'Or at Cannes and an Academy Award. Its lush imagery, and soundtrack by Antonio Carlos Jobim and Luiz Bonfá, make one pine for the Rio of fifty years ago.

# J

## JIU-JITSU

Developed from Japanese judo, Brazilian jiu-jitsu is a martial art predicated on the idea that one can overcome a stronger and bigger opponent by using leverage and other techniques. Not that size is an issue for twin brothers and jiu-jitsu champions Antônio Rodrigo and Antônio Rogério Nogueira.

# B

## BAIANA

Residents of the state of Bahia have a distinct culture influenced by their African roots. Baiana women, with their flowing dresses and head wraps, have been paid tribute by singers including Gilberto Gil, Carmen Miranda, and the percussion group Barbatuques.

# M

## MAYRINK VEIGA, CARMEN

Brazil's quintessential society doyenne and fashion icon, Carmen Mayrink Veiga has been painted by Andy Warhol, Pablo Picasso, and Candido Portinari. She has also been photographed by Richard Avedon, Mario Testino, and Francesco Scavullo; in 1981 she was inducted into *Vanity Fair*'s best-dressed list.

# G

## GABEIRA, FERNANDO

This politician and journalist took part in the kidnapping of the American ambassador to Brazil in 1969, in protest of his country's military regime. He eventually went into exile, and scandalized his countrymen when he was photographed wearing a tiny knit bikini bottom upon his return.

# G

## GABEIRA, MAYA

Surfing is a big deal in Brazil, and no one in the sport is a bigger deal than Maya Gabeira, Fernando Gabeira's daughter. In 2009 she surfed a forty-five-foot wave in South Africa—the largest ever by a female.

# M
## MOSAICS

The abstract stone mosaic boardwalk that runs alongside Copacabana beach is one of Roberto Burle Marx's masterpieces. Seen from the tall buildings across the street, it resembles a single, four-mile-long canvas.

# S

## SEGRETO, CONRADO

Despite showing only five collections, Conrado Segreto, who died of AIDS in 1992 at the age of thirty-two, had an outsize impact on Brazilian fashion. His couturelike dresses were a hit among São Paulo's society women, and he helped invigorate the local luxury market at a time of deep economic crisis.

# P

## PINK DOLPHINS

Even the wildlife in Brazil seems to have an innate sense of style. Toucans and parrots flaunt their gaudy plumage in the treetops, but underwater, in the Amazon River, the pink dolphin is surely the chicest animal

# M.

## METROPOLIS

São Paulo is one of the most congested cities in the world, with a population of about twenty million— and growing. Seen up close, its rows of cell-like apartments bring to mind a modernist beehive.

# N
## NORTHEASTERN FACADES

The colorful facades and lyrical geometry of the humble houses in villages all over Brazil's northeastern region are some of the most important examples of vernacular architecture anywhere. Their esthetic impact proudly defies their inhabitants' lack of material wealth.

# C
## COPACABANA

Bookended by two historic forts and flanked by Roberto Burle Marx's curving promenade resembling black and white waves, Copacabana is Rio's most popular beach. Every New Year's Eve, the entire city converges there to party.

# V

## VELOSO, CAETANO

Aside from being one of Brazil's most revered musicians, Caetano Veloso was one of the founders of the *tropicália* movement and a committed political activist. During the 1960s the military government censored his songs and eventually sent him to prison. Veloso was forced into exile for two years, but upon his return in 1972 became a bigger star than ever.

# F
## FIO DENTAL

Minimalist fashion in Brazil means wearing as little as possible. On the beach, this translates into "dental floss" bikinis for women, which leave the buttocks almost fully exposed. In a country where beautiful bodies are considered an essential part of the culture, less (clothing) is definitely more.

# COPACABANA PALACE

The Copacabana Palace is one of the most legendary hotels in the world. Its design was inspired by the Negresco in Nice and the Carlton in Cannes, and it has hosted celebrities and dignitaries ranging from Ava Gardner and Orson Welles to Prince Charles and Bill Clinton.

# D

## DOCES BÁRBAROS

Doces Bárbaros was the group formed in the 1970s by, from left, Gilberto Gil, Maria Bethânia, Gal Costa, and Caetano Veloso. They each had successful individual careers, but came together to tour, produce a record (now considered a masterpiece of Brazilian music), and to make a documentary, which was released in 1977.

# T
## TROPICÁLIA

Also known as *tropicalismo*, tropicália was an artistic and musical movement from the 1960s that fused Brazilian culture with avant-garde influences. This poster, designed by Rogério Duarte for Glauber Rocha's 1964 *cinema novo* film *Deus e o Diabo na Terra do Sol*, is emblematic of the graphic, colorful motifs used in tropicália record covers and film posters.

# S

## SALLES, WALTER, JR., AND MONTENEGRO, FERNANDA

The son of a prominent diplomat and banker, Walter Salles, Jr., is one of Latin America's most respected directors, thanks to films like *The Motorcycle Diaries* and *Central Station*. For the latter, Fernanda Montenegro became the first Brazilian actress to be nominated for an Academy Award.

# D

## DINIZ, LEILA

When the outspoken actress Leila Diniz declared in a 1969 interview that "It's possible to love one person and go to bed with another—it's happened to me," the military government censored all magazines and newspapers. Diniz died in 1972, at the peak of her fame, in a plane crash in India.

# R

## ROCHA, MARTHA

The controversy over Martha Rocha, Miss Brazil 1954, proved how seriously Brazilians take beauty pageants. She came in second at Miss Universe despite being the front-runner, allegedly because her curvy hips and bottom were a tad too large for the standards of the time.

# C

## CAPOEIRA

African slaves in Brazil developed this combination of dance and martial arts as a way to train body and mind for combat. Although it was once forbidden, capoeira is now celebrated as a national sport and has gained a global following.

# A
## ARCOS DA LAPA

Built in the eighteenth century, this aqueduct located in the center of Rio brought water from the Carioca River to the city. The Lapa neighborhood is now a booming party destination, filled with samba clubs.

# S
## SANTOS-DUMONT, ALBERTO

This coffee heir and aviation pioneer circled the Eiffel Tower in a dirigible in 1901, and made the first European public flight in an airplane in 1906. Cartier designed its now famous Santos wristwatch in Santos-Dumont's honor, so he could easily check the time while flying.

# J

## JABUTICABA

Also known as Brazilian grapes, jabuticaba can be used for medicinal purposes and to make jellies and drinks. But this fruit, indigenous to the Minas Gerais province, is most famous thanks to the song of the same name by Bebel Gilberto.

# C
## CITY OF GOD

Fernando Meirelles's 2002 film *City of God* tracks the evolution of a group of criminal favela kids in Rio from the 1960s to the 1980s. Using handheld cameras and nonprofessional actors, Meirelles confronted the general public with some of Brazil's most disturbing social problems.

# I
## IPANEMA

Thanks to Antonio Carlos Jobim and Vinicius de Moraes's song "The Girl From Ipanema," few places in the world are more famous than the stretch of sand between Arpoador and Leblon. The tune was written in 1962, but fifty years later Ipanema is still a magnet for the most beautiful people in Rio.

# I
## IEMANJÁ

In Brazil's Afro-American Candomblé religion, Iemanjá is the goddess of the ocean, protector of fishermen and shipwrecked sailors. She is especially worshiped in the state of Bahia, but in Rio, on New Year's Eve, throngs of devotees spiffily attired in white converge on Copacabana beach to place flowers and other offerings on the waves.

# T

## THAT MAN FROM RIO

It's not a masterpiece of filmmaking, but *That Man From Rio,* a 1964 spy spoof starring Jean-Paul Belmondo, showed European audiences beautifully shot images of then exotic places like Rio, Brasília, and the Amazon.

# T
## TELENOVELAS

Dramatic television soap operas are an essential part of Brazilian culture. One of the all-time favorites is 1976's *Escrava Isaura* (pictured), about a light-skinned slave's difficult quest for happiness during the Brazilian empire. It was broadcast in over eighty countries.

# P

## POPOZUDAS

In many societies, large breasts are considered the ultimate in sex appeal; for Brazilians, the backside has place of honor. "Popozudas" is the nickname given to women who are naturally endowed with arresting derrieres (sometimes with the aid of butt-lifting Brazilian jeans), such as the funk dancer and singer Grace Kelly de Olivera Souza (pictured).

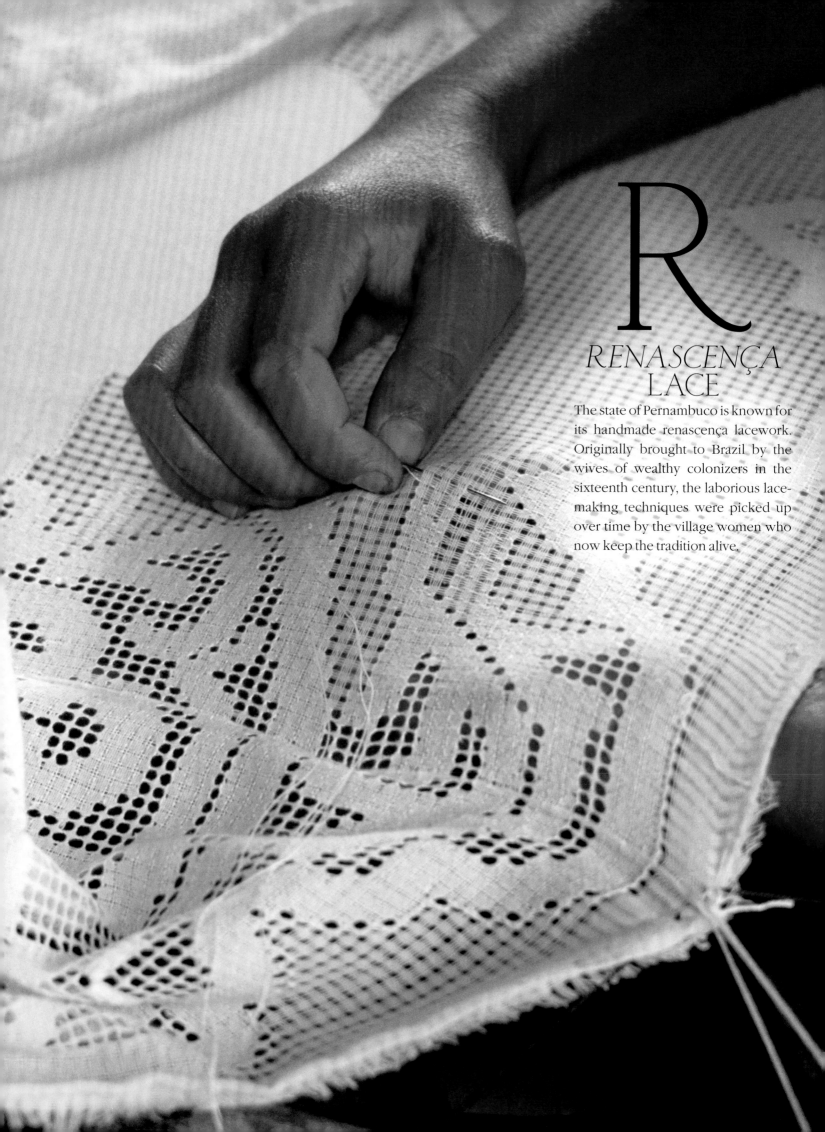

# R
## RENASCENÇA LACE

The state of Pernambuco is known for its handmade renascença lacework. Originally brought to Brazil by the wives of wealthy colonizers in the sixteenth century, the laborious lace-making techniques were picked up over time by the village women who now keep the tradition alive.

# M
## MOQUECA

This famous fish and seafood dish has existed in Brazil for centuries. Unlike most stews, it is cooked without any water, using palm oil and coconut milk instead.

# A
## ATALA, ALEX

Before becoming his country's most famous (and most tattooed) chef, Alex Atala was a punk and a deejay. He ushered in a new era of Brazilian gastronomy, reinventing traditional local dishes with modern techniques and indigenous ingredients.

# M

## MIELE, CARLOS

Carlos Miele's forte is unabashedly sexy gowns and swimwear that incorporate traditional artisanal techniques like patchwork, stitching, and crochet. His bold colors, slit-up-to-there hemlines, and plunging necklines have made him a red-carpet regular.

# M
## MANAUS

Located in the heart of the Amazon, Manaus is best known for its magnificent Teatro Amazonas opera house, depicted in Werner Herzog's film *Fitzcarraldo*. Built with considerable difficulty at the end of the nineteenth century, it was outfitted with Murano chandeliers, Carrara marble columns, French furnishings, and a dome decorated with 36,000 tiles painted in the colors of the Brazilian flag.

# C
## COLLECTIVE WEDDINGS

For ages, collective weddings have offered couples with limited resources the chance to band together and tie the knot in one large ceremony, in order to not break the bank.

# F
## FASANO

Since 1902, when Vittorio Fasano, a Milanese immigrant, arrived in São Paulo and opened the Brasserie Paulista, the Fasano family has been leading the way in gastronomy and hospitality. Aside from the Fasano hotel in São Paulo (pictured), the empire now includes hotels in Rio and Boa Vista in Brazil, and Punta del Este, Uruguay, as well as ten restaurants.

# B
## BUARQUE, CHICO

Like many other musicians, writers, and poets of the 1960s, Chico Buarque was detained by the military. In the famous song "Cálice," a duet with Milton Nascimento, he used the homophony between the word "chalice" in Portuguese and *cale-se*—which means "shut up"—to protest the dictatorship's censoring of free speech.

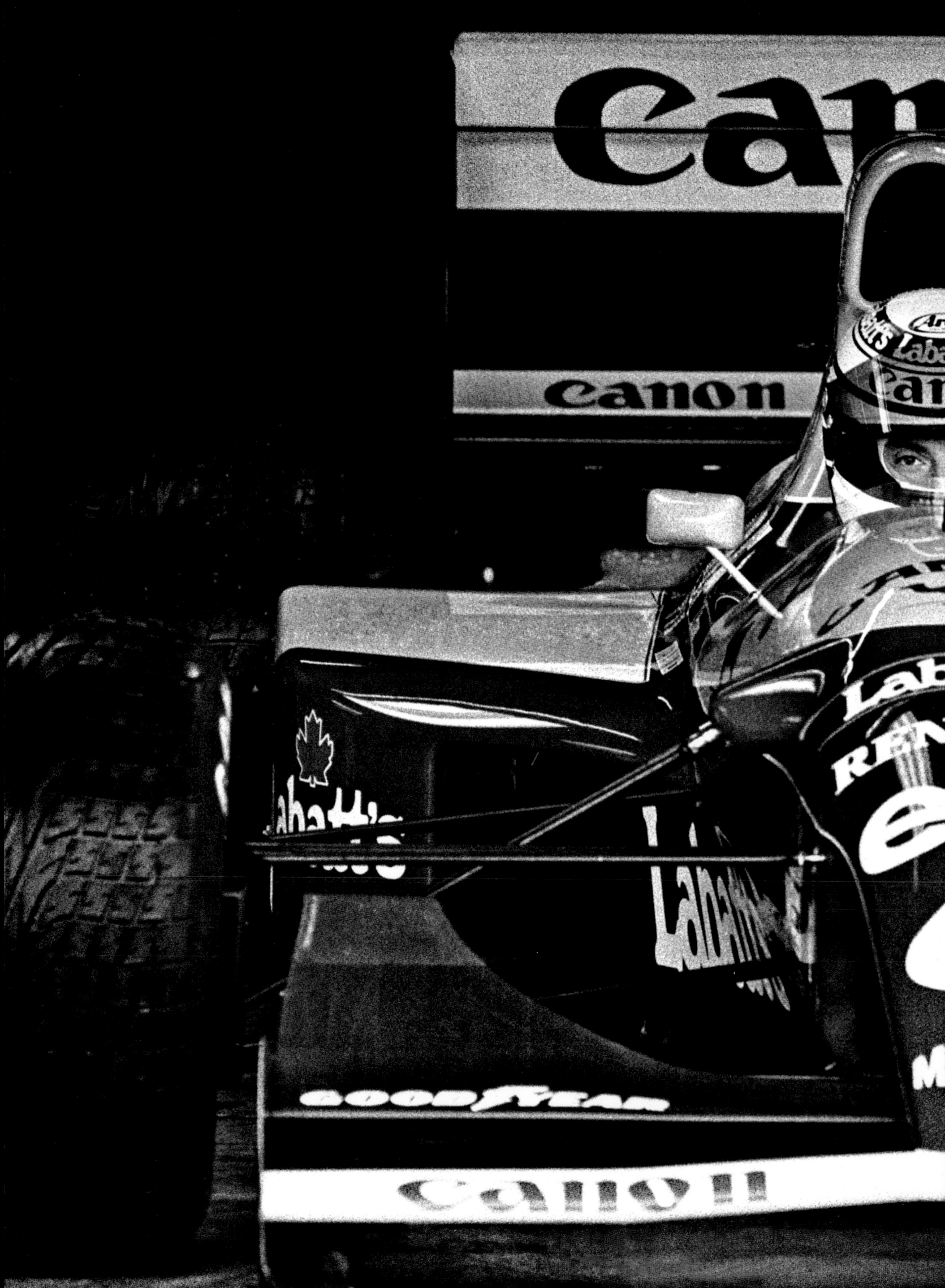
Canon
GOODYEAR

# F

## FORMULA 1

Brazilian race-car drivers like Ayrton Senna, Nelson Piquet, and Emerson Fittipaldi are some of the most glamorous Formula 1 champions ever. Success comes with a price, however: Ayrton Senna died in a crash during the San Marino Grand Prix in 1994.

# H
## HAVELANGE, JOÃO

He served as president of FIFA, the International Football Association Federation, from 1974 to 1998, but João Havelange is a sportsman as much as an executive, having competed in the 1936 Olympic Games as a swimmer and in the 1952 Games as part of the Brazilian water polo team; he joined the International Olympic Committee in 1963 and is currently its longest serving member.

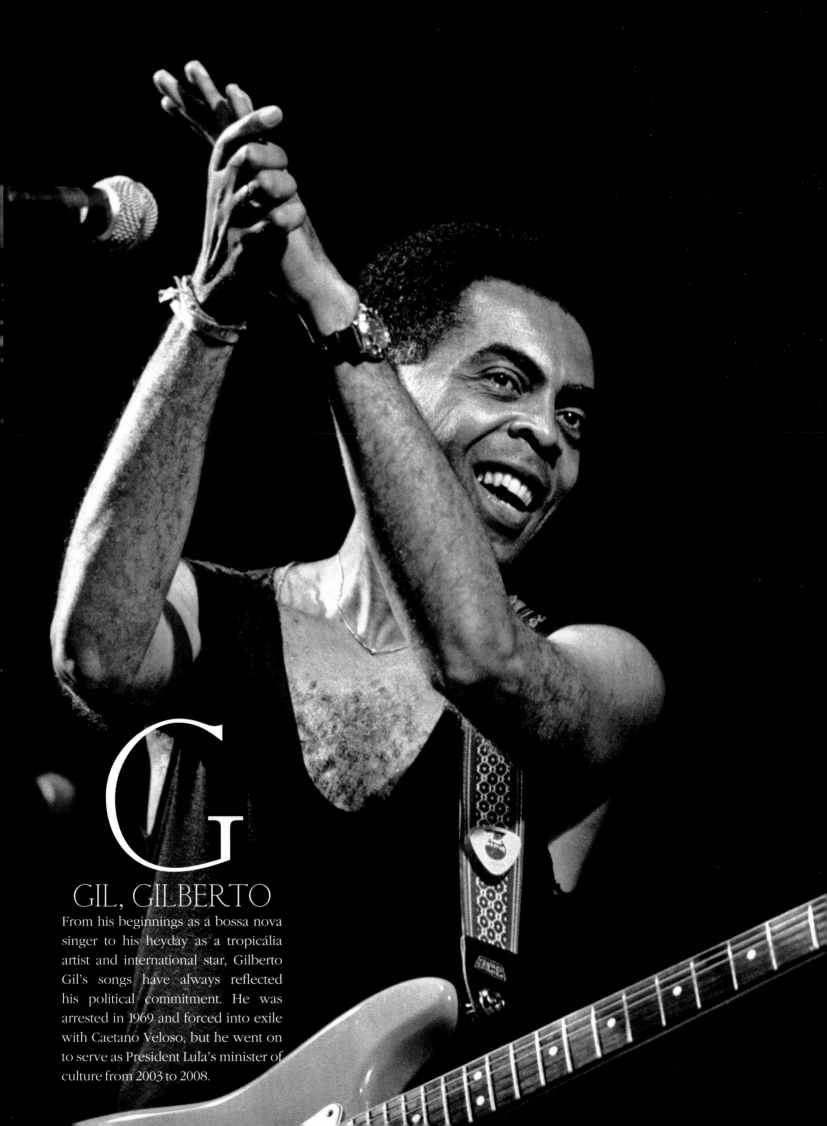

# GIL, GILBERTO

From his beginnings as a bossa nova singer to his heyday as a tropicália artist and international star, Gilberto Gil's songs have always reflected his political commitment. He was arrested in 1969 and forced into exile with Caetano Veloso, but he went on to serve as President Lula's minister of culture from 2003 to 2008.

# C
## CACHAÇA AND CAIPIRINHA

Anyone who's had a caipirinha—the dangerously delicious cocktail served just about everywhere in Brazil—knows they pack quite a punch. Their secret is cachaça, the liquor made from sugar cane. The variety of cachaça labels shown at left proves just how popular the spirit is.

To make Brazil's national drink:
1-2 tsp granulated sugar
1-2 limes, quartered
2.5 oz cachaça of your choice
1 cup ice cubes
Crush and muddle the lime wedges with sugar in a large glass, using a wooden pestle or spoon. Add cachaça and fill with ice. Stir well. Drink at your own risk.

# E

## EDIFÍCIO COPAN

Oscar Niemeyer's undulating Edifício Copan, in downtown São Paulo, is one of the most famous symbols of modernism in the world. But for Paulistas, the building is just as important because of the Café Floresta—a standing-room-only coffee shop where, for decades, locals have stopped by for coffee, orange juice, and the cheese puffs known as *pão de queijo*.

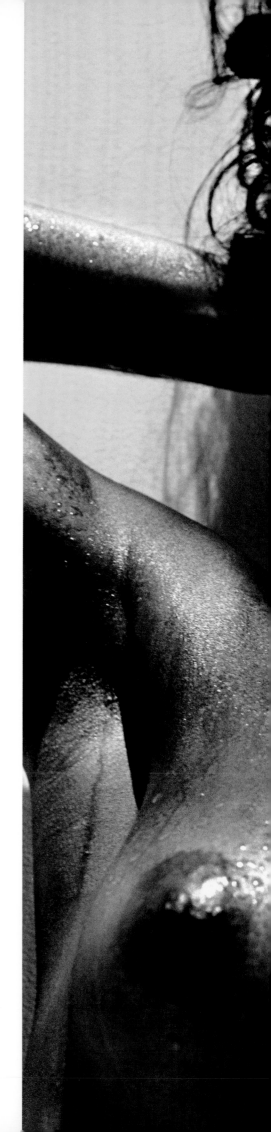

# B

## BRAGA, SONIA

She made a name for herself starring in the soap
opera *Gabriela,* but bombshell Sonia Braga
became an international sex symbol thanks to
her saucy performance in the 1976 film *Doña
Flor and Her Two Husbands,* based on the novel
by Jorge Amado. She went on to appear in
critically acclaimed movies such as *Kiss of the
Spider Woman* and *The Milagro Beanfield War.*

# M

## MART'NÁLIA

Music is in Mart'nália's blood: Her father, Martinho da Vila, is a famous sambista, and her mother, Analia Mendonça, is a singer (Mart'nália's name is an amalgam of her parents'). The performer, songwriter, and percussionist started out in Rio nightclubs, and now tours in Europe and Africa.

# A
## AÇAÍ

People in the Amazon have been consuming açaí for centuries, well before this little fruit became the object of a global health craze. Due to its increasing demand, açaí trees have been used to replant some degraded areas of the Amazon.

# J
## JAPANTOWN

Brazil is home to the largest Japanese population outside of Japan, and in Liberdade, São Paulo's Japantown, one can see how intertwined the two cultures have become. During Carnaval, there are even Japanese-themed samba tributes.

# H

## HAVAIANAS

Despite their name, Havaianas come from Brazil, not Honolulu. The first pair was created in 1962, inspired by zori, the traditional Japanese sandals. Since then, the casual flip-flops have become a wardrobe staple in practically every beach town around the world.

# C

## CAMPANA BROTHERS

Working with everything from wood scraps and cardboard to stuffed animals, Fernando and Humberto Campana transform ordinary materials into extraordinary furniture. Their low-tech approach to design is consistent with the way many Brazilians with scant means but rich imaginations instinctively recycle discarded goods.

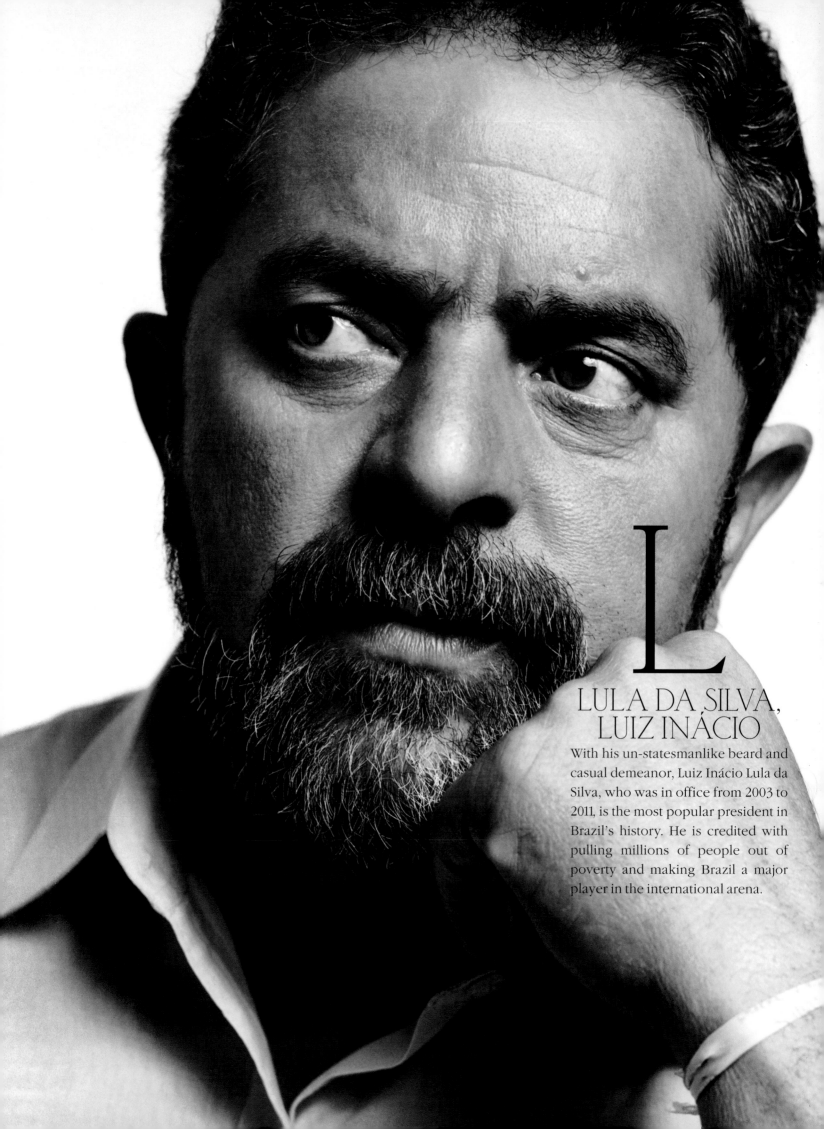

# L

## LULA DA SILVA, LUIZ INÁCIO

With his un-statesmanlike beard and casual demeanor, Luiz Inácio Lula da Silva, who was in office from 2003 to 2011, is the most popular president in Brazil's history. He is credited with pulling millions of people out of poverty and making Brazil a major player in the international arena.

# P

## PORTINARI, CANDIDO

Brazilians think of Candido Portinari as their greatest painter ever. He literally gave his life to producing epic works that captured his country's soul. Even though doctors had warned him that exposure to paint was killing him, he carried on and died of lead poisoning in 1962.

# A
## *ACARAJÉ*

What to eat while you're on the go, checking out the sights in Salvador? Try acarajé—black-eyed peas seasoned with dried shrimp and onions, deep-fried in palm oil, then split and filled with a spicy shrimp paste.

# A

## ASSUME VIVID
## ASTRO FOCUS

Assume Vivid Astro Focus is both artist Eli Sudbrack's alias and the name of his international art collective, which he helms with French artist Christophe Hamaide Pierson. Whether it's paintings, drawings, photography, film, or digital technology, AVAF's work is characterized by its pulsating, psychedelic energy.

# T
## TRIBES

It is estimated that at the beginning of the sixteenth century there were about two thousand different indigenous tribes in Brazil. Many of these died out as a consequence of European settlement, while others became assimilated. Still, according to some reports, Brazil currently has the highest number of uncontacted native populations in the world.

# K
## KRAJCBERG, FRANS

Nature is both the subject and the raw material for this sculptor, photographer, and painter. His wooden creations using mangrove trees draw attention to problems like deforestation, making them as much an ecological statement as an artistic one.

# B
## BURLE MARX, ROBERTO

The late Roberto Burle Marx's gardens, tapestries, drawings, sculptures, and public architecture blended cubism and abstract expressionism with landscape design. Thanks to him, Brazil's astounding diversity of flora can be seen in an artistic context.

# C
## COLONIAL
## ARCHITECTURE

To purists, Brazilian colonial architecture may feel like a bit of a mish-mash. Despite this, many Brazilian buildings, like this church in Olinda, in the state of Pernambuco, are some of Latin America's best reflections of the prevailing European styles of the time.

# R
## ROCKS
Portuguese for "general mines," the aptly named state of Minas Gerais has huge reserves of semiprecious stones, including aquamarines, topazes, and tourmalines (pictured).

# H
## H. STERN

Hans Stern, a German immigrant who arrived in Brazil at age seventeen, founded H. Stern in 1945, when the colored gemstone trade was virtually nonexistent. By the time of his death in 2007, he had created a global jewelry empire with 170 stores in twenty-six countries.

# V

## VAREJÃO, ADRIANA

She was married to Bernardo Paz, the collector who founded the Inhotim museum, but Adriana Varejão is one of Brazil's leading contemporary artists in her own right. Using typical elements like pottery and the blue Portuguese tiles known as *azulejos,* her work often alludes to the breakdown of colonialism.

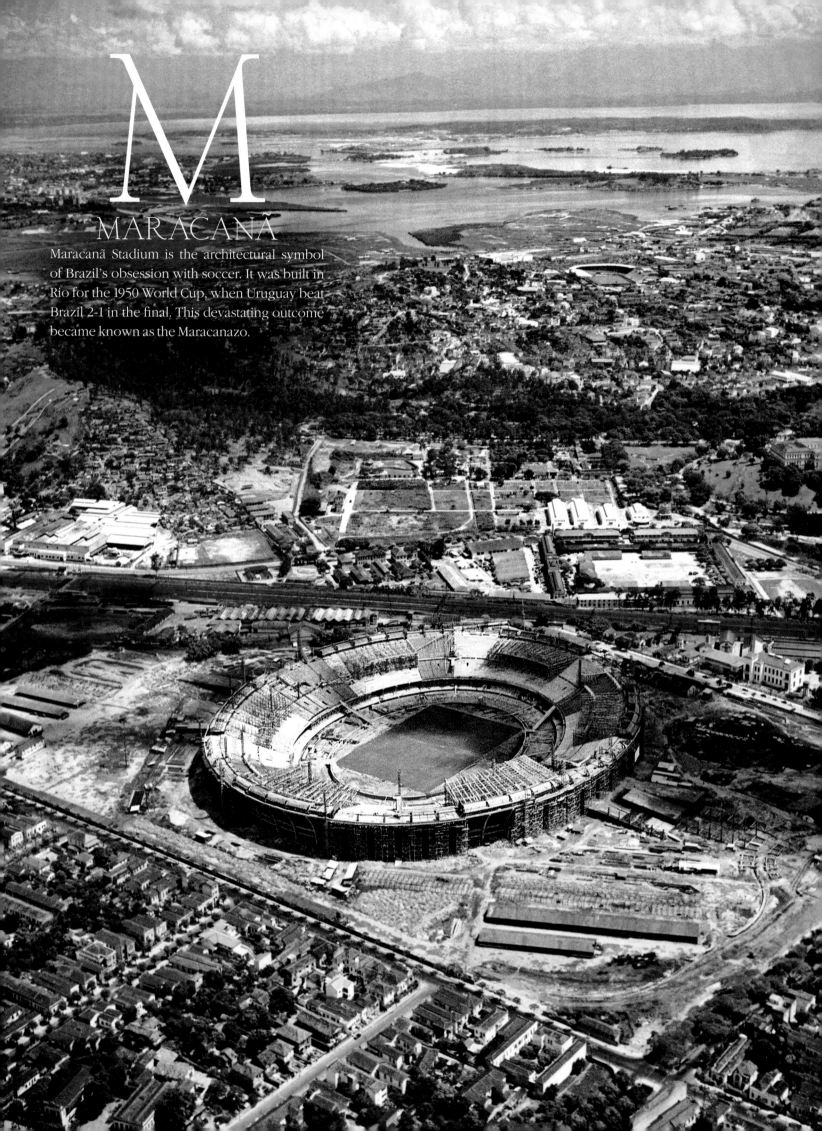

# M
## MARACANÃ

Maracanã Stadium is the architectural symbol of Brazil's obsession with soccer. It was built in Rio for the 1950 World Cup, when Uruguay beat Brazil 2-1 in the final. This devastating outcome became known as the Maracanazo.

# X

## XUXA

Reportedly the wealthiest Brazilian entertainer, Xuxa got her start as a model in the 1970s, went on to pose for *Playboy,* and dated Pelé and race-car driver Ayrton Senna. She has starred in a multitude of movies and released many albums, but it was her children's television show, *Xou da Xuxa,* which ran from 1986 to 1993 and showed her emerging from a pink spaceship, that made her a superstar.

# V

## VOLLEYBALL

In parts of Brazil, volleyball rivals football in popularity—even supermodel Gisele had dreams of becoming a professional competitor. Since the 1980s, Brazilian volleyball teams have been snapping up top medals in the Olympics and other international competitions. They've had good training: If you take a stroll down any Brazilian beach, chances are you'll eventually find a game in progress.

# B
## BRAZILIAN WAX

Undoubtedly the country's most painful export, Brazilian waxing involves complete hair removal from the pelvic region, presumably in order to wear the tiniest thong imaginable. No pain, no gain.

# M
## MENDES DA ROCHA, PAULO

Winner of the Pritzker Architecture Prize in 2006, Paulo Mendes da Rocha emerged as the unofficial leader of Brazil's avant-garde brutalist architecture movement in the 1950s. His most famous works, such as São Paulo's Brazilian Sculpture Museum, make concrete and steel look like sculptural materials.

# M

## MUNIZ, VIK

To make his art, Vik Muniz has worked with chocolate syrup, diamonds, and, recently, trash. For his Pictures of Garbage series (pictured), he made monumental portraits out of refuse, depicting the workers in a Rio landfill; the images were sold at auction, with the proceeds used to support the workers' cooperative.

# A
## ANGEL, ZUZU

Zuleika Angel Jones, known as Zuzu, was a Brazilian-American fashion designer whose activist son was "disappeared" by the military. She embarked on a quest to recover his body—which was never found—but was killed in a car crash in 1976. Years later, after Brazil became democratic, the government admitted that the regime of the time had been involved in her death.

# I
## INCENSE

The use of incense is common in most religions, but followers of Umbanda, which mixes Catholicism with spiritism, have far more options than traditional sandalwood. Believers can purchase varieties specifically designed to, among other things, "attract wealth," "avoid the evil eye," and, for the especially prudent, "protect yourself against everything."

# R

## RUA AUGUSTA

The prevailing attitude in the Rua Augusta is that sex is good—and easy to find. For years this street has been the epicenter of São Paulo's red-light district, though in recent times the area has also seen an influx of trendy clubs and restaurants.

# M

## MIRANDA, CARMEN

Although she was born in Portugal, Carmen Miranda was nothing but Brazilian. The samba-singing, hip-swirling bombshell crafted an instantly recognizable image that relied on platform shoes, massive headpieces, and swingy dance ensembles that were sometimes worn without underwear.

# Z

## ZÉ CARIOCA

José Carioca, a dapper parrot from Rio de Janeiro, was Donald Duck's good friend. He starred in Disney's 1942 film *Saludos Amigos*, and had a cameo in *Who Framed Roger Rabbit*.

# J

## JOBIM, ANTONIO CARLOS

Tom Jobim, as he is popularly known, was instrumental in developing the bossa nova style. Several of his songs were written with the poet and diplomat Vinicius de Moraes, but he truly became a worldwide star after his collaborations with Stan Getz, João Gilberto, and Gilberto's wife Astrud, who sang on "The Girl From Ipanema."

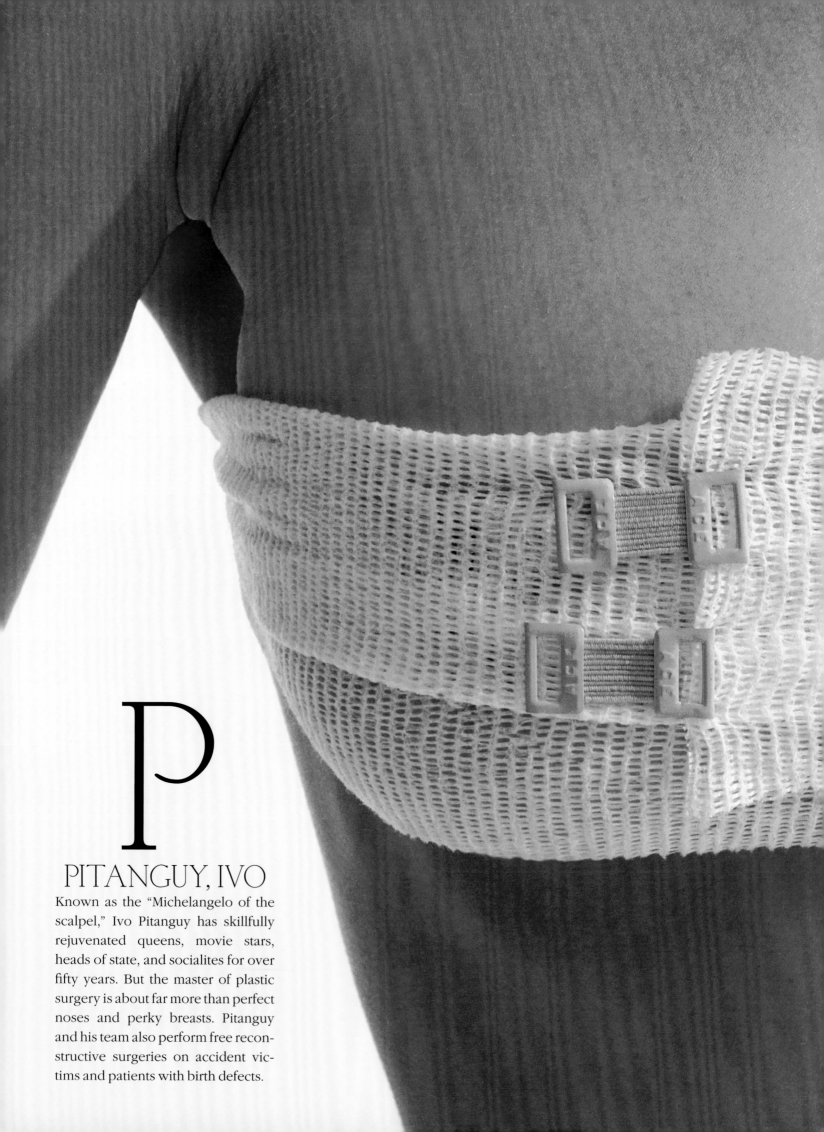

# P

## PITANGUY, IVO

Known as the "Michelangelo of the scalpel," Ivo Pitanguy has skillfully rejuvenated queens, movie stars, heads of state, and socialites for over fifty years. But the master of plastic surgery is about far more than perfect noses and perky breasts. Pitanguy and his team also perform free reconstructive surgeries on accident victims and patients with birth defects.

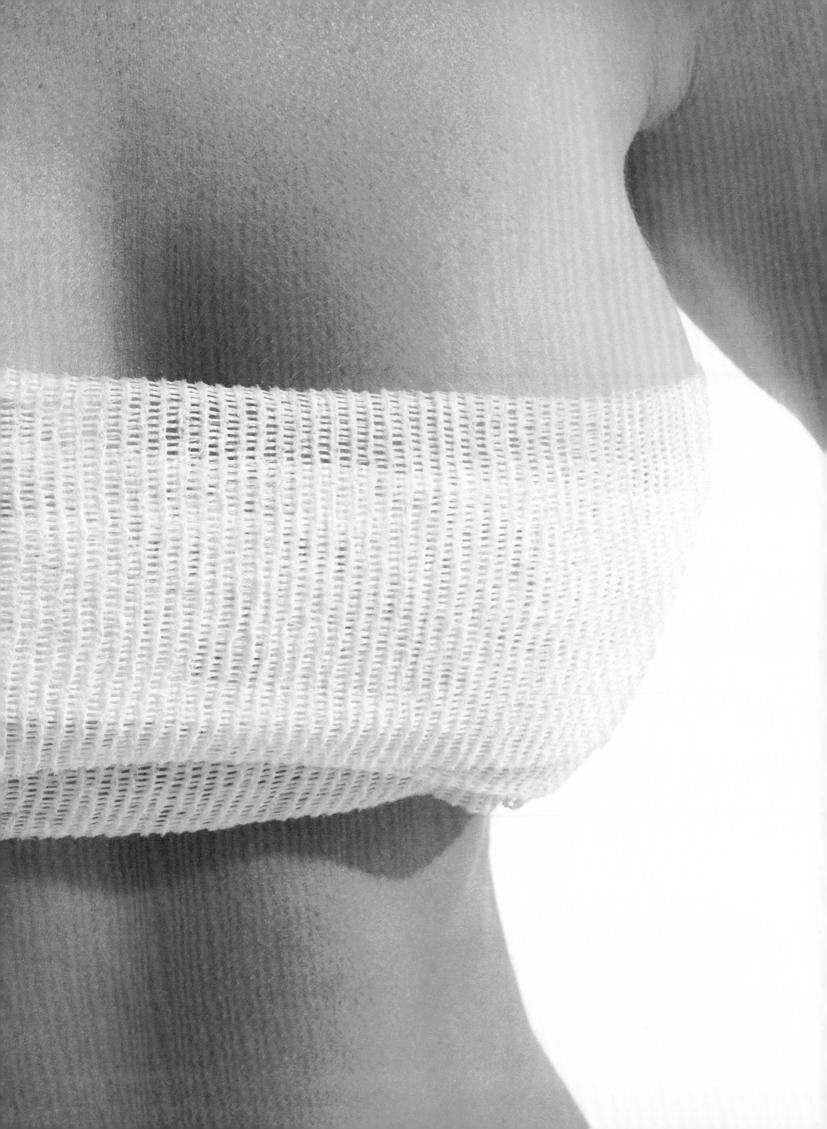

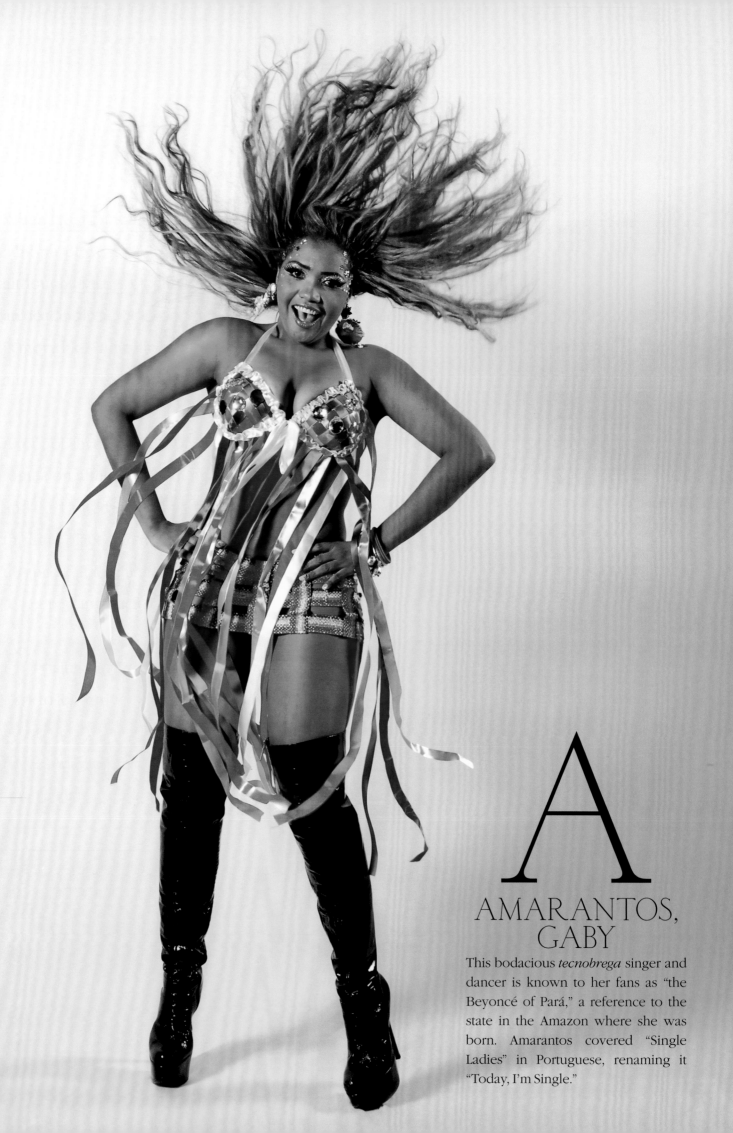

# A
## AMARANTOS, GABY

This bodacious *tecnobrega* singer and dancer is known to her fans as "the Beyoncé of Pará," a reference to the state in the Amazon where she was born. Amarantos covered "Single Ladies" in Portuguese, renaming it "Today, I'm Single."

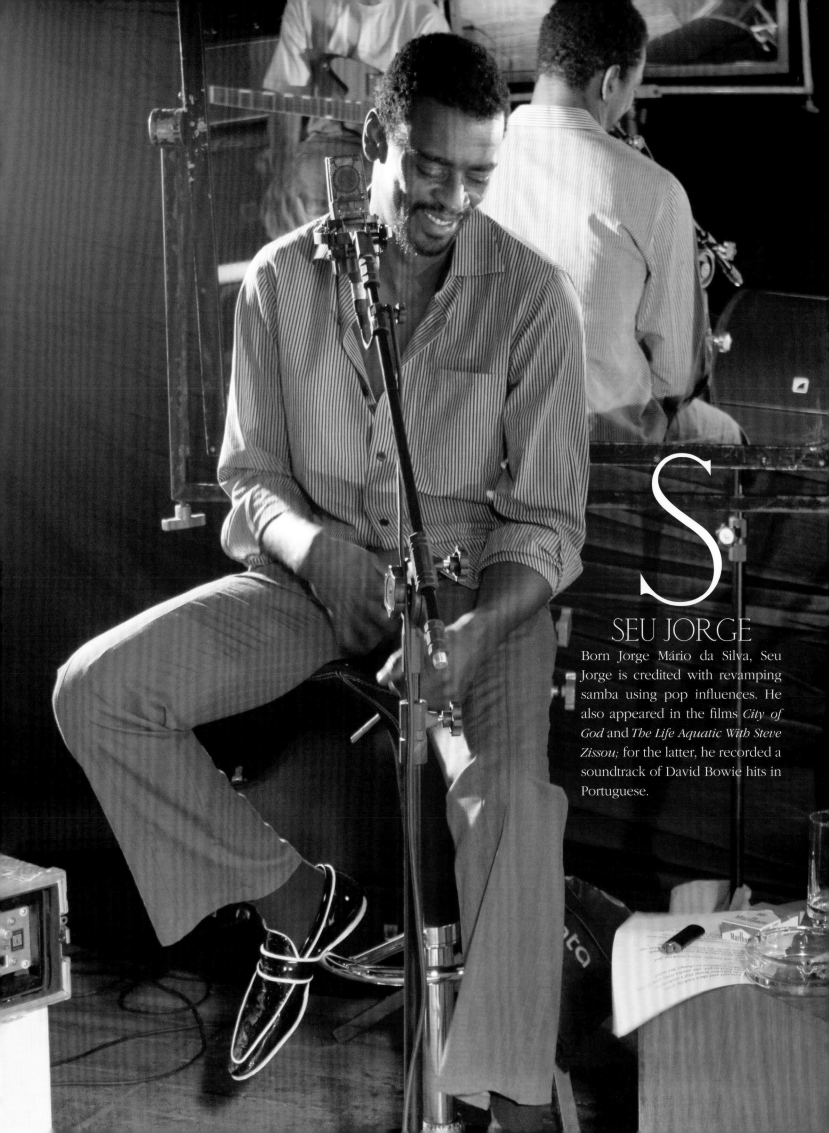

# S

## SEU JORGE

Born Jorge Mário da Silva, Seu Jorge is credited with revamping samba using pop influences. He also appeared in the films *City of God* and *The Life Aquatic With Steve Zissou;* for the latter, he recorded a soundtrack of David Bowie hits in Portuguese.

# Y

## YES, BRAZIL

Simão Azulay brought a punky, new-wave edge to 1980s fashion with Yes, Brazil, which he founded in 1979. The label, known for its jeans and prints, became a favorite of the Brazilian band Blitz (pictured).

# C

## COSTA, FRANCISCO

Judging by the spiffy mini-tuxedo he's wearing in this childhood family picture, fashion was always in Francisco Costa's blood. For the past eight years he has been the coolly minimalist women's creative director of Calvin Klein Collection, but few people know that he grew up on a ranch in Guarani and started out designing decidedly un-minimal costumes for Carnaval.

# I

## INDIGENOUS
## MEDICINE

Healing potions made from fruit, bark, and other natural elements have always been used in Brazil. Interest in these alternative remedies is growing within the medical establishment, which has begun to recognize that the rain forest's immense biodiversity could hold the cure for many diseases.

# F
## FAVELA

The Brazilian shantytowns known as favelas have well documented problems: drugs, violence, and poverty. But they are also vibrant and full of possibilities. For his *Women Are Heroes* project, which was meant to call attention to women in troubled areas, the French artist JR plastered steps in Rio's Morro da Providência favela with this massive portrait.

# DOM PEDRO

The son of King John VI of Portugal, Dom Pedro I declared Brazilian independence on September 7, 1822, and was subsequently crowned emperor. His reign was short-lived, though: He abdicated in favor of his five-year-old son in 1831.

# H
## HELICOPTERS

São Paulo has one of the biggest helicopter fleets in the world. Weekday mornings, as businesspeople commute to work high in the sky to avoid the traffic-clogged streets, the city resembles an episode of *The Jetsons*.

# TIRADENTES

Joaquim José da Silva Xavier, known as Tiradentes, or "Teeth-puller," was a leader of Brazil's independence movement in the eighteenth century. He was arrested and hanged, and his body was dismembered and publicly exhibited to dissuade protesters. After Brazil became a republic in 1889, the anniversary of his death became a national holiday, and there is now a city named after him.

A JOAQUIM JOSÉ DA SILVA XAVIER
HEROI MAIOR DA NACÃO BRASILEIRA
HOMENAGEM DE SUA TERRA NATAL
1792-1992

PREFEITO EM EXERCICIO
LUIZ JOSE DA FONSECA
PRESIDENTE DA CAMARA
JOSE ANTONIO DO NASCIMENTO

# F
## FEIJOADA

Originally from Portugal, feijoada is Brazil's national dish. A bean stew with pork, rice, manioc flour, and assorted sausages, it's mercifully served only for lunch, on Sundays, and on special occasions.

# I
## INHOTIM

Inhotim is a three-thousand-acre outdoor museum near Belo Horizonte devoted to contemporary art. The brainchild of collector Bernardo Paz, it houses large-scale works by Doug Aitken, Chris Burden, Matthew Barney, Hélio Oiticica, Doris Salcedo, and Jarbas Lopes (pictured), among others.

## GUARANÁ

A powerful natural stimulant containing about twice the caffeine of coffee, guaraná is widely consumed in Brazil, especially in sodas. These are so popular that some brands are now being exported to Portugal and Spain.

# P
## POMERODE

German and Germanic dialects are still spoken in Pomerode, a small town in the south of Brazil where Pomeranian immigrants settled in 1861. The residents have held on to their vernacular architecture and traditional customs ever since.

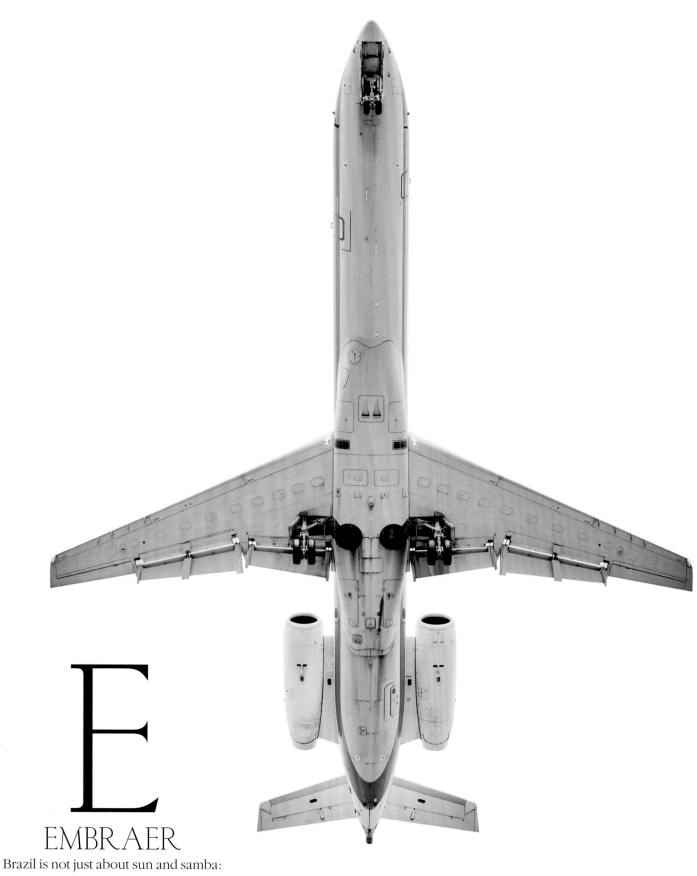

# E

## EMBRAER

Brazil is not just about sun and samba:
By some accounts, it is the fifth largest
economy in the world. Companies
like Embraer, which manufactures
airplanes, prove that the country can
compete in high-tech arenas.

# C

## CORCOVADO

The statue of Christ the Redeemer overlooking Rio from atop Corcovado peak is one of the country's most emblematic symbols; so much so that it appears on everything from beach towels to this caftan, created by the swimwear designer Adriana Degreas.

# V

## VALE DO AMANHECER

Mystical beings, extraterrestrials, ancient Egyptian beliefs, and Jesus Christ are all important influences for the Valley of Dawn religious sect, headquartered about fifty kilometers from Brasília. Judging by some of their ensembles, debutante balls may also be a subconscious source of inspiration.

# R

## RUBBER

The global demand for rubber sourced from the Amazon generated a huge economic boom at the turn of the twentieth century in cities like Belém and Manaus. However, the need for an extensive labor force to physically extract latex from the trees led to the enslavement and gross mistreatment of the local populations.

# N

## NASCIMENTO, MILTON

When he was eighteen months old, Milton Nascimento's mother, who was a housekeeper, died. He was adopted by her employers, and went on to become a major influence in Brazilian popular music. His famous song "Coração de Estudante" ("Student's Heart") became a hymn for the Diretas Já political movement of the 1980s, which demanded democratic elections and eventually led to the end of the military regime.

# I

## IGUAÇU FALLS

Located on the border between Brazil and Argentina, Iguaçu Falls—150 million years old and plunging sixty-five meters with a width of almost three kilometers—puts Niagara Falls to shame. Appropriately, the name means "big water" to the local Guaraní Indians who have inhabited the area for more than 2,000 years.

# V

## VICTORIA REGIA

These floating Amazonian plants are like Monet's water lilies on tropical steroids. They can grow circular leaves with a diameter of up to ten feet—big enough for a small child to sit on without sinking.

# L
## LEONILSON

José Leonilson was a painter and sculptor whose powerful career was cut short by AIDS in 1993, at age thirty-six. His early work was ebullient, colorful, and confident, while his later pieces turned toward intimacy and melancholy, using spare canvases marred with stitching to reflect his feelings of vulnerability.

# S

## SAMBA

There is no stronger symbol of Brazilian national identity than samba. Like Brazil itself, the famous hip-swinging musical genre is in constant evolution: Over the years, variations such as samba-funk, samba-rock, and samba-reggae have emerged, mostly in the favelas.

# C

## CARNAVAL

Held from the Saturday to the Tuesday before Ash Wednesday, Brazil's Carnaval, with public samba performances and processions in all major cities, practically paralyzes the country. The massive celebration originated as a last indulgence in music, food, alcohol, and sex before the abstinence of Lent: In Latin, *carne vale* means "farewell to the flesh."

# N

## NAKAO, JUM

The grandson of Japanese immigrants, Jum Nakao brings together the worlds of art, fashion, and design to create memorable experiences. During one of his performances, the models showing his exquisitely ephemeral paper dresses, reminiscent of historical costumes, ripped them to shreds on the catwalk, even though they had taken hundreds of hours to make.

# OSKLEN

Oskar Metsavaht, a sports medicine specialist, founded his Osklen label in 1989, after climbing Mont Blanc wearing athletic gear of his own design. The label, which has since expanded internationally, retains a sporty, ecological bent.

# B
## BRASÍLIA

Brazil has only recently become a global power, but it's been dreaming big since 1956, when Lúcio Costa and Oscar Niemeyer planned and built the country's modernist capital. It is the seat of government and diplomacy, but the city's main draw is its architectural masterpieces.

# B

## BARROCO BRASILEIRO

Catholic missionaries introduced baroque art to Brazil in the seventeenth century as a tool for Christian indoctrination. Churches like São Francisco (pictured), in Salvador, are the epitome of gaudy splendor, rivaling even their most ornate European counterparts.

# M
## MONTE, MARISA

Combining influences as disparate as jazz, soul, bossa nova, samba, and rock, Marisa Monte emerged as Brazil's most eclectic singer of the 1990s. She has collaborated with artists including Ryuichi Sakamoto and David Byrne.

# COOPA-ROCA

Sociologist Maria Teresa Leal started this cooperative in the 1980s as a way of helping women in Rio's poorest neighborhoods to make a living. Teaming up with labels like Carlos Miele and Osklen, members of Coopa-Roca handcraft decorative elements that are used in high-end clothes.

# D
## DASLU

What began as a small family business in 1958 had evolved into Brazil's most luxurious department store by the turn of the twenty-first century. Socialites, magnates, and celebrities arrived at Daslu—sometimes by helicopter—to purchase the latest European fashion collections while being tended to by squadrons of uniform-wearing maids.

# L
## LENÇÓIS MARANHENSES

Most of Brazil is teeming with lush vegetation, but the Lençóis Maranhenses National Park, located in Maranhão state, is just the opposite. At first sight its dunes, which stretch for about a thousand square kilometers, look like a typical desert, but during the rainy season they are dotted with blue and green freshwater lagoons.

# S

## SUNGA

The masculine counterpart to women's fio dental thongs is the sunga. Not to be confused with the Speedos that professional swimmers favor, sungas are made of heavier nylon and are cut to form a nearly horizontal band across the body.

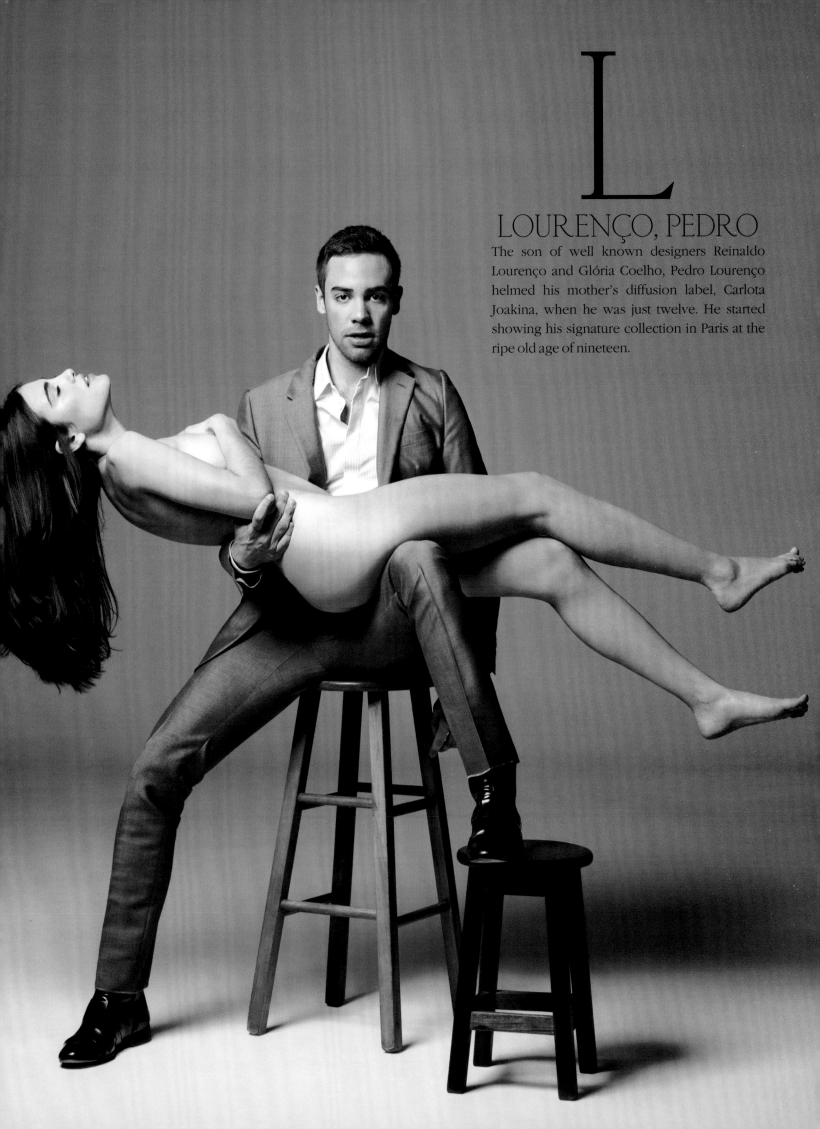

# L
## LOURENÇO, PEDRO

The son of well known designers Reinaldo Lourenço and Glória Coelho, Pedro Lourenço helmed his mother's diffusion label, Carlota Joakina, when he was just twelve. He started showing his signature collection in Paris at the ripe old age of nineteen.

# H
## HERNANDES, CLODOVIL

Clodovil Hernandes's career path was anything but predictable. He started out as a fashion designer during the 1960s and '70s; became a famous television presenter, whose over-the-top, right-wing views often landed him in hot water; and was elected as Brazil's first openly gay congressman in 2006. He suffered a fatal stroke three years later.

# F

## FALCHI, CARLOS

In the 1970s, no disco princess's outfit was complete without a sexy Carlos Falchi handbag swinging from her shoulder. The leather wizard made ensembles for everyone from Cher to Tina Turner—and his accessories have recently been spotted on the likes of Katy Perry and Rihanna.

# M
## *MARACATÚ*

This musical performance genre sprang from the Reis do Congo ceremonies of colonial times, in which slaves anointed leaders within their own communities. The processions, popular in the state of Pernambuco, now include characters imitating the royal Portuguese court of the sixteenth century, and in the Cearense version of Maracatú, practiced in Fortaleza, transvestites in blackface play the most important female roles.

# C

## CANDOMBLÉ

The most popular Afro-Brazilian religion, Candomblé originated in Salvador, the capital of Bahia, which was the center of the slave trade in colonial times. During Candomblé ceremonies, priests fall into a trancelike state while invoking Yoruban deities known as Orixás.

# F

## FORRÓ

Samba and bossa nova may be internationally acclaimed, but in northeastern Brazil, it's all about forró—the equivalent of country music. In cities like Recife and Fortaleza, bands playing accordions, triangles, and *zabumba* drums regularly draw thousands of fans.

# D

## DELLAL, ANDREA

She is the fabulous matriarch of Brazil's First Fashion Family. A former model (nicknamed "Rio"), Dellal passed on plenty of chic genes to her daughters: Charlotte is a successful accessories designer whose label, Charlotte Olympia, is shown in Paris; Alice, who was once dubbed the "punk debutante" by *The New York Times,* plays in a band, models, and is the business partner of the jeweler Dominic Jones.

# J

## JOELMA

Few performers of *brega,* a hard-hitting genre of popular music, are more adored than Joelma, who goes by her first name only, and makes up Banda Calypso with her husband, Chimbinha. The exuberance of her voice and dance moves is rivaled only by that of her wardrobe.

# R

## RODRIGUES, SERGIO

Along with Joaquim Tenreiro, Jorge Zalszupin, and José Zanine Caldas, Sergio Rodrigues brought mid-century Brazilian design to the international arena. He is known for his use of native woods such as jacaranda, and the unusual contours of his stuffed leather chairs and sofas.

# OITICICA, HÉLIO

This key figure of the neo-concrete art movement, who died in 1980 at age forty-two of a stroke, worked with everything from abstract paintings to sculptures and interactive installations. His wearable art pieces, known as *parangolés,* were meant for samba parades or moments of private reverie, as Oiticica demonstrated in a video.

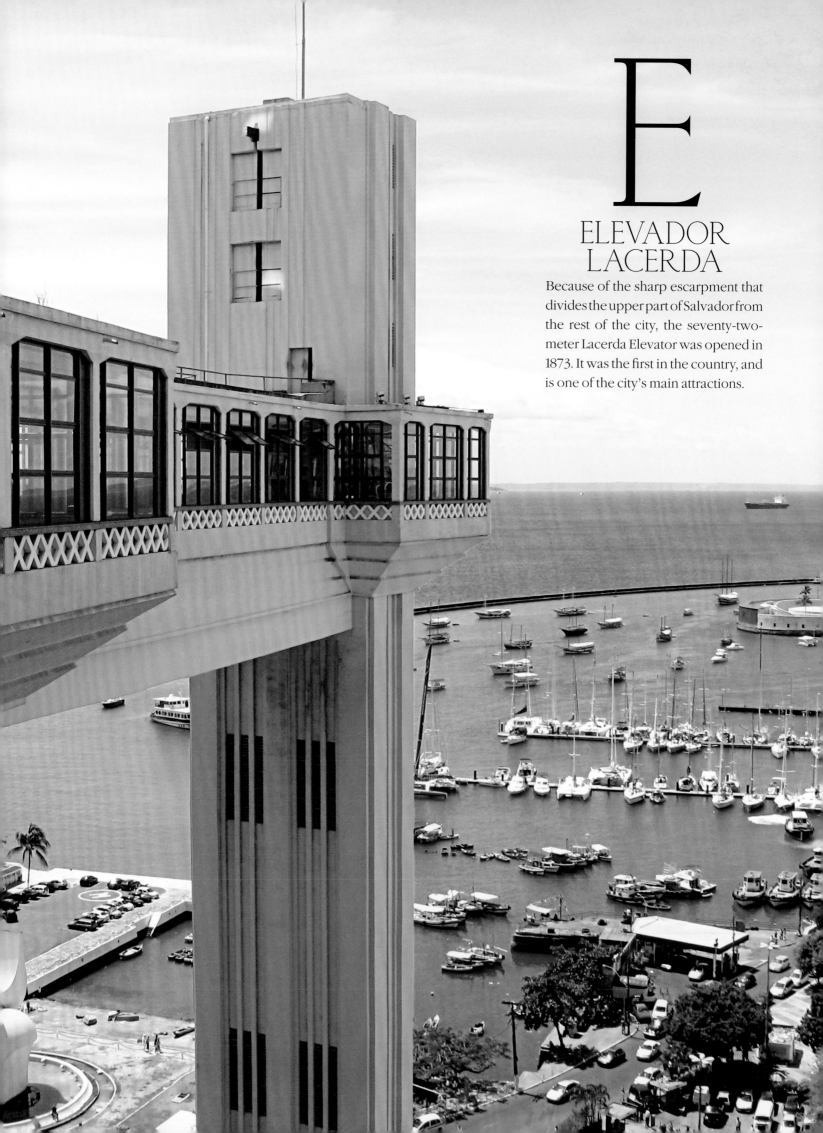

# E

## ELEVADOR LACERDA

Because of the sharp escarpment that divides the upper part of Salvador from the rest of the city, the seventy-two-meter Lacerda Elevator was opened in 1873. It was the first in the country, and is one of the city's main attractions.

# N

## NIEMEYER, LENNY

The Brazilian swimwear industry is one of the biggest in the world, and few people have helped it gain recognition abroad like Lenny Niemeyer. The niece by marriage of architect Oscar Niemeyer, Lenny—as she is known to pretty much everyone in Rio—launched her business in 1993 and quickly became the queen of the beach by transforming traditional swimsuits into chic fashion statements with sexy straps, artful embellishments, and splashy prints.

# CANGACEIROS

Cangaceiros were leather-clad gangs of bandits who rejected the dominance of landowners and roamed the northeast of Brazil during the late nineteenth and early twentieth centuries. Their romanticized, antiestablishment mythology inspired films such as 1953's *O Cangaceiro* (pictured).

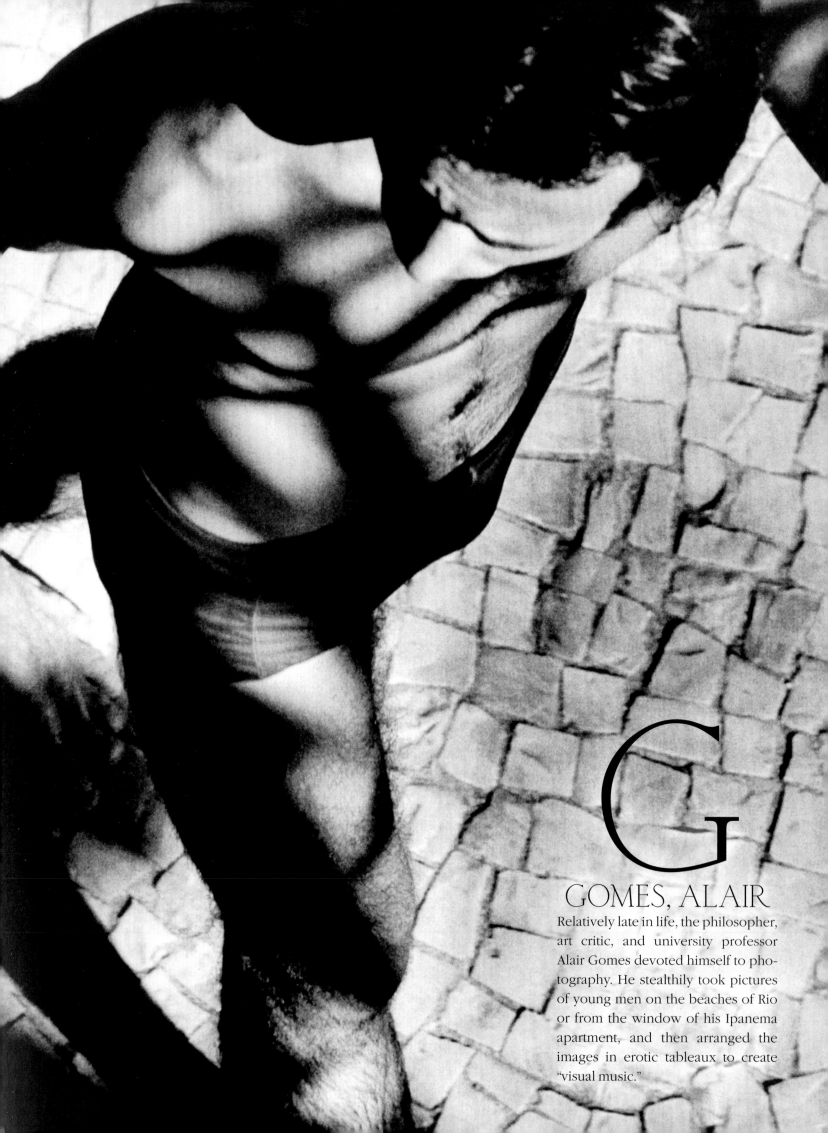

# G

## GOMES, ALAIR

Relatively late in life, the philosopher, art critic, and university professor Alair Gomes devoted himself to photography. He stealthily took pictures of young men on the beaches of Rio or from the window of his Ipanema apartment, and then arranged the images in erotic tableaux to create "visual music."

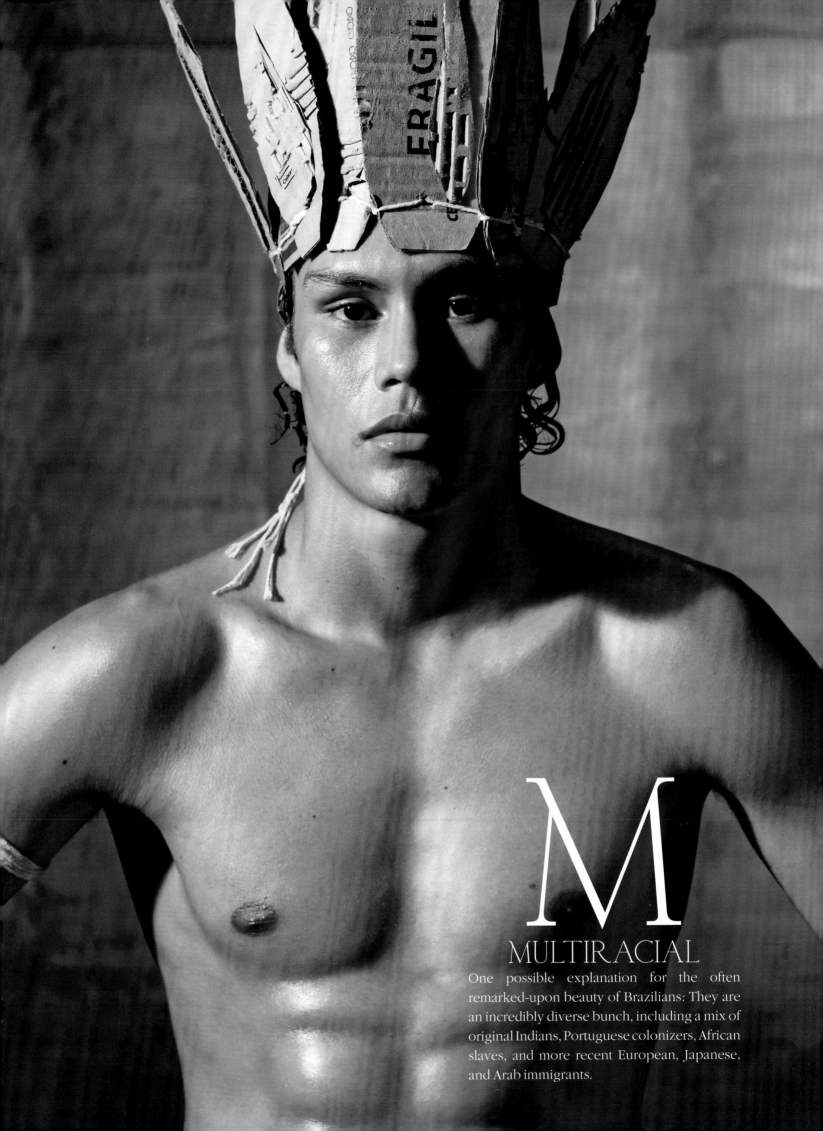

# M

## MULTIRACIAL

One possible explanation for the often remarked-upon beauty of Brazilians: They are an incredibly diverse bunch, including a mix of original Indians, Portuguese colonizers, African slaves, and more recent European, Japanese, and Arab immigrants.

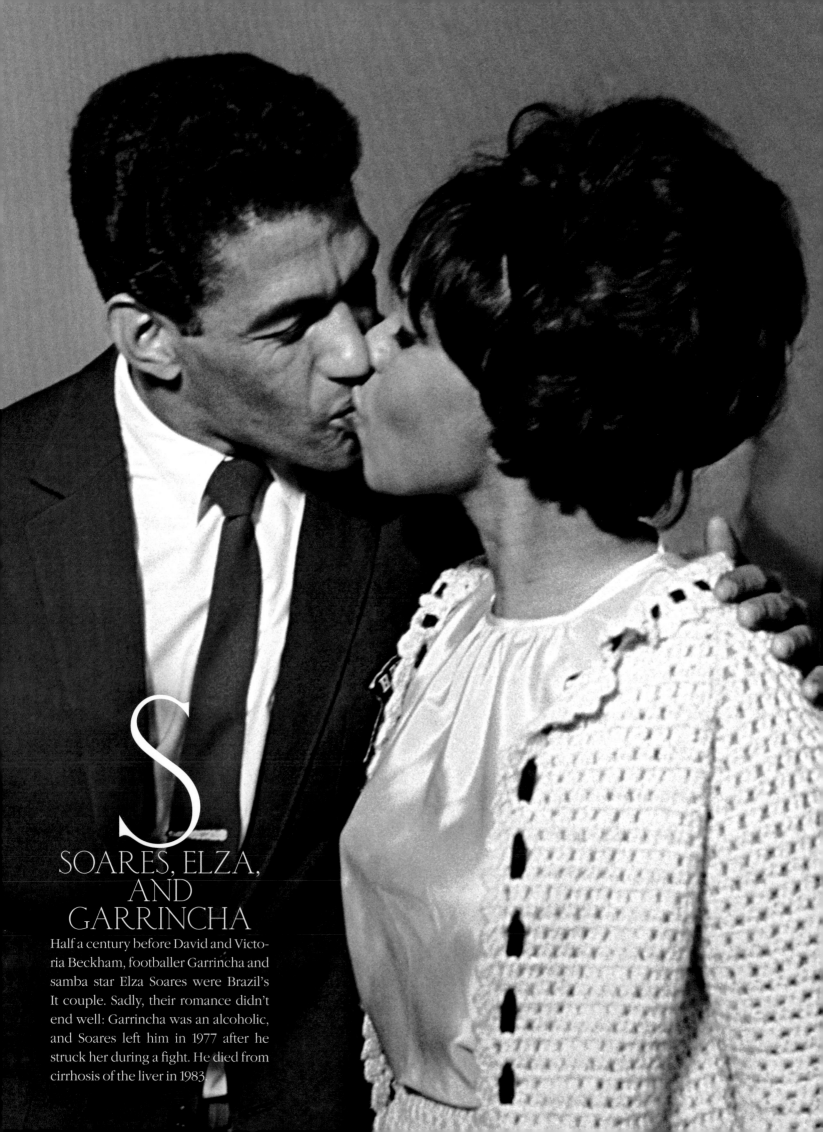

# SOARES, ELZA, AND GARRINCHA

Half a century before David and Victoria Beckham, footballer Garrincha and samba star Elza Soares were Brazil's It couple. Sadly, their romance didn't end well: Garrincha was an alcoholic, and Soares left him in 1977 after he struck her during a fight. He died from cirrhosis of the liver in 1983.

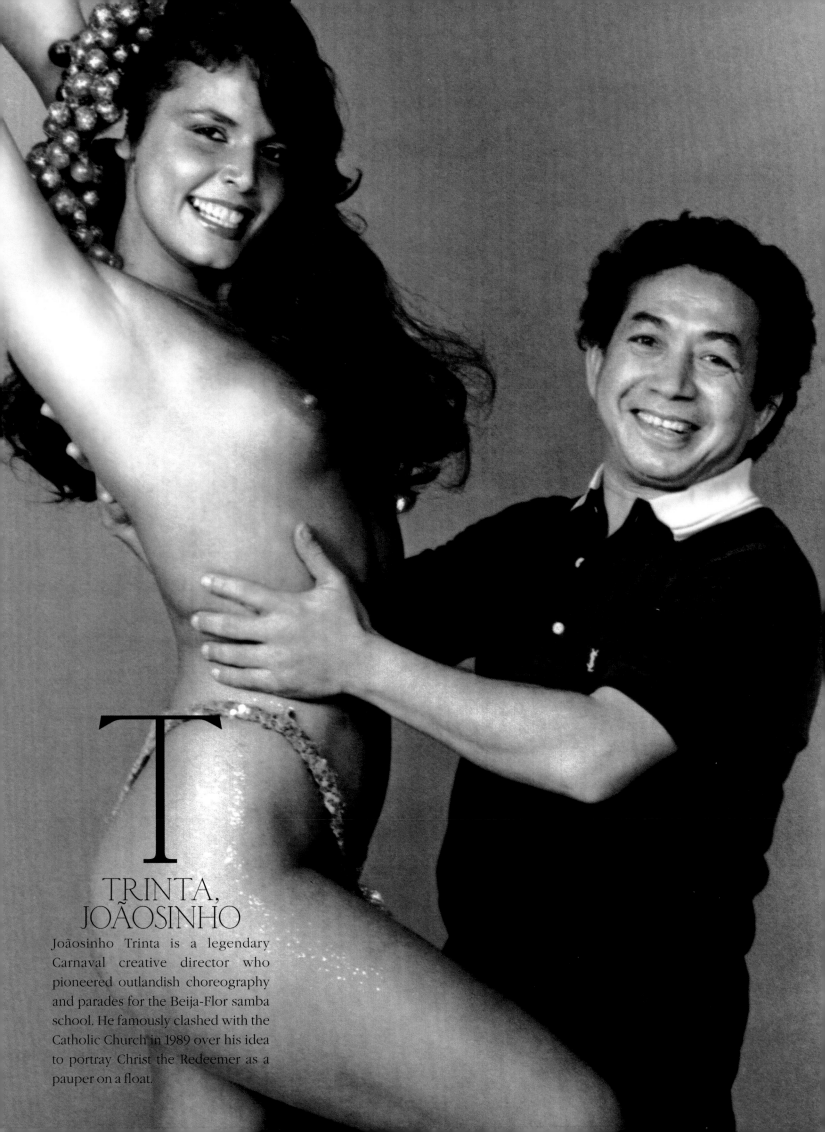

# T

## TRINTA, JOÃOSINHO

Joãosinho Trinta is a legendary Carnaval creative director who pioneered outlandish choreography and parades for the Beija-Flor samba school. He famously clashed with the Catholic Church in 1989 over his idea to portray Christ the Redeemer as a pauper on a float.

# D

## DENER

During the 1950s and '60s, Dener Pamplona de Abreu was Brazil's pre-eminent couturier. The champagne-swilling tropical dandy, who died of cirrhosis in 1978, was famous not just for dressing the chicest women of his time but also for his withering maxims, such as "I hate fat and indecisive women," and "I'm the Coco Chanel of Brazilian fashion."

# CARIOCA

## S

### SANTA TERESA

Although Rio is invariably associated with its beaches, the hilly neighborhood of Santa Teresa is being developed with beautiful residential hotels. The coolest (though not fastest) way to get there is aboard the tram—the only one in Rio—that winds all the way to the top from the center of the city.

GOVERNO DO
**Rio de Janeiro**
SECRETARIA DE TRANSPORTES

03

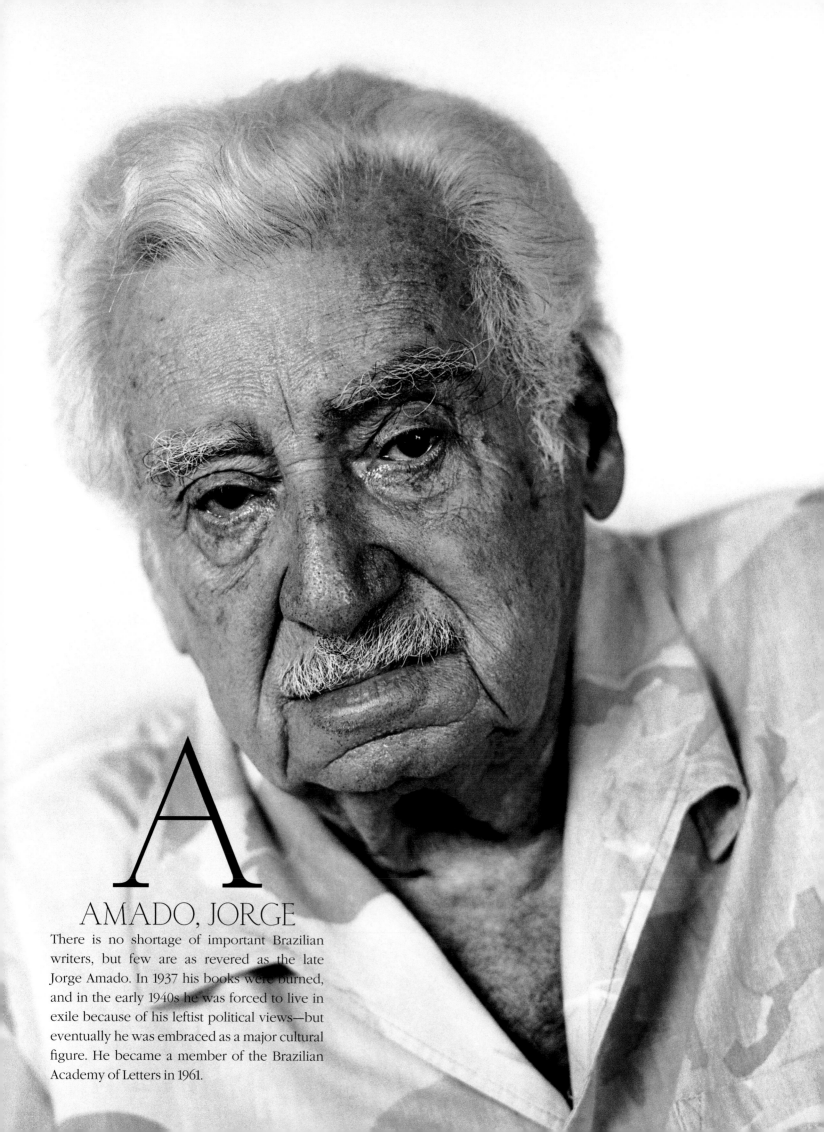

# A
## AMADO, JORGE

There is no shortage of important Brazilian writers, but few are as revered as the late Jorge Amado. In 1937 his books were burned, and in the early 1940s he was forced to live in exile because of his leftist political views—but eventually he was embraced as a major cultural figure. He became a member of the Brazilian Academy of Letters in 1961.

# A

## ARAÚJO, WALÉRIO

His outlandishly bombastic designs are not for the faint of heart, which is why Brazilian starlets—not to mention gender illusionists and attention-seeking night revelers—worship at the altar of Walério Araújo.

# B

## *BRIGADEIRO*

These mouth-size chocolate balls, created in the 1940s in honor of the presidential candidate (and brigadier) Eduardo Gomes, are to Brazil what cupcakes are to the United States. This simple recipe makes about twenty brigadeiros.

3 tbsp unsweetened cocoa
1 tbsp butter
1 14-oz can condensed milk

Combine all ingredients in a saucepan over medium heat. Stir for about ten minutes, until mixture is thickened. Let rest and form into small balls when cool enough to handle.

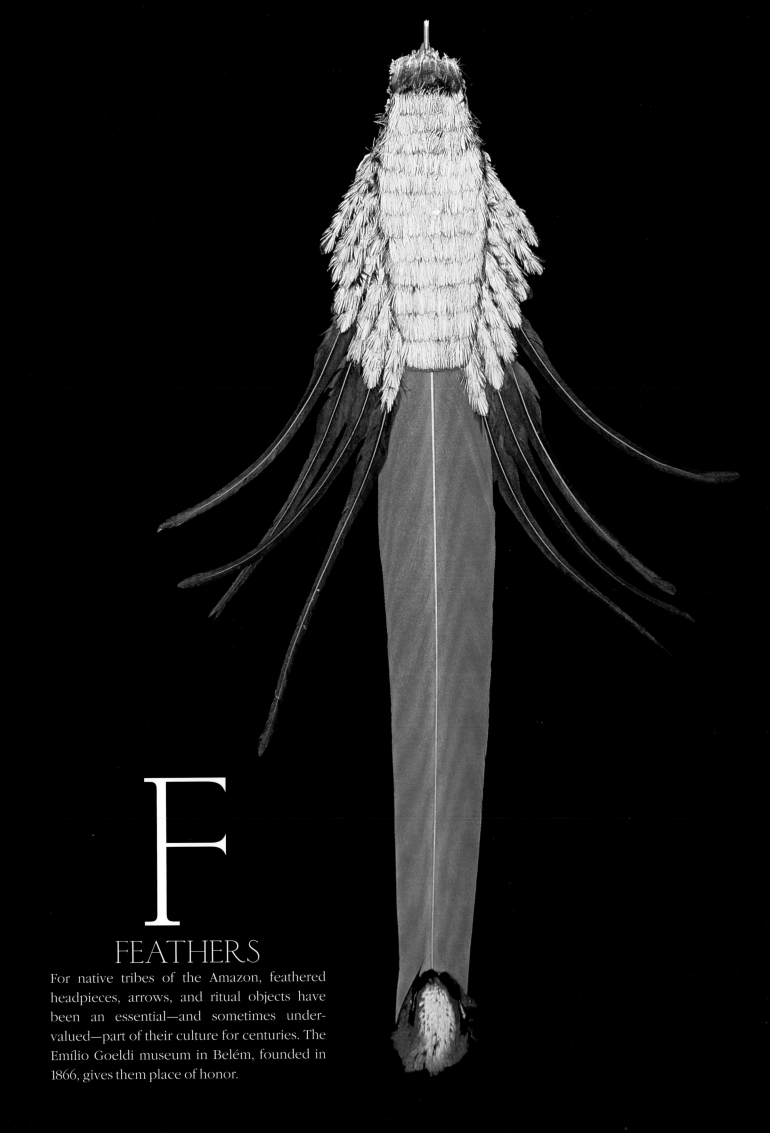

# F
## FEATHERS

For native tribes of the Amazon, feathered headpieces, arrows, and ritual objects have been an essential—and sometimes under-valued—part of their culture for centuries. The Emílio Goeldi museum in Belém, founded in 1866, gives them place of honor.

# P
## PORTO MARAVILHA

Rio is in the process of rehabilitating its port district in time for the 2016 Olympics. The urban development plan includes new parks and squares, an aquarium and art gallery, and the futuristic Museum of Tomorrow, designed by the starchitect Santiago Calatrava.

# L
## LIFEGUARDS
Watching the lifeguards in Rio exercise in the morning may prompt some bathers to purposely swim out a bit too far.

# W

## WONDER, CLAUDIA

This outré transsexual performer, who passed away in 2010, was a militant gay activist, punk singer, theater and film actress, and magazine columnist. Wonder was also the subject of several documentaries, including 2009's *My Buddy Claudia*, by Dácio Pinheiro.

# B
## BECKER, CACILDA

In 1969, forty-eight-year-old Cacilda Becker, one of Brazil's most respected and beloved stage actresses, suffered a stroke during a performance of *Waiting for Godot* and died 38 days later. A theater in São Paulo was named in her honor in 1988.

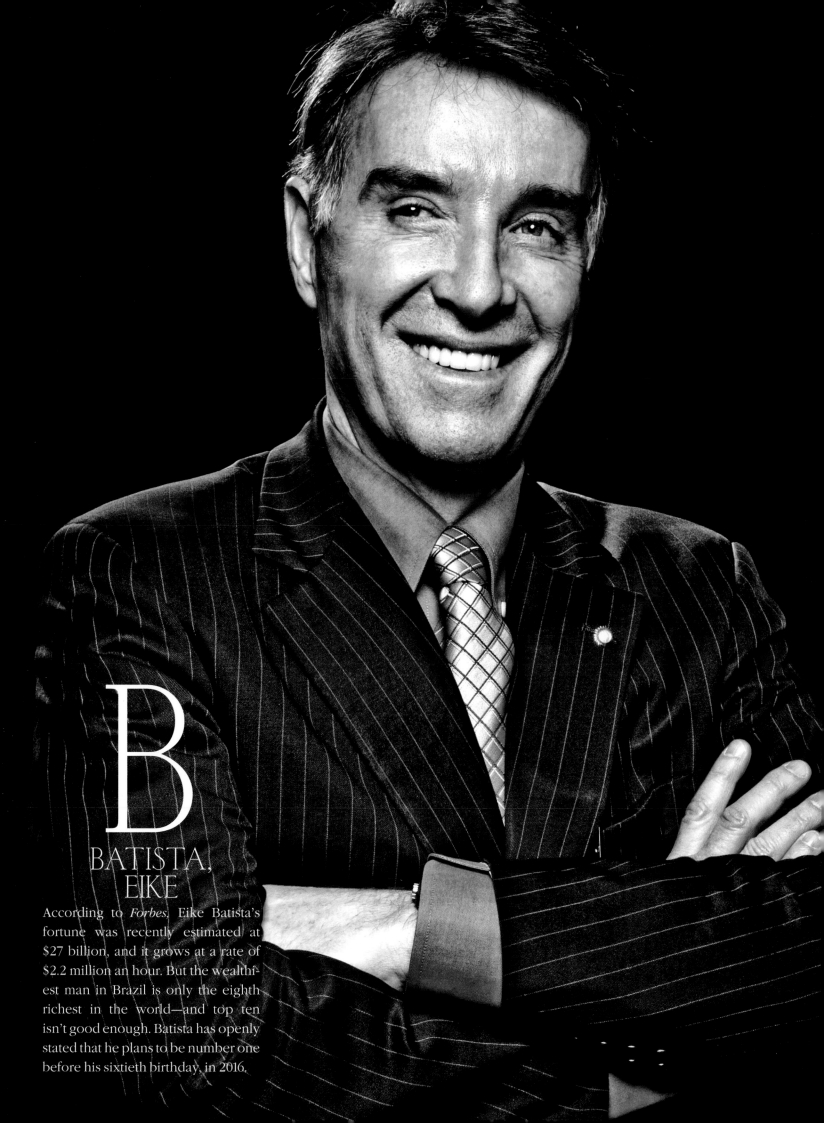

# B
## BATISTA, EIKE

According to *Forbes*, Eike Batista's fortune was recently estimated at $27 billion, and it grows at a rate of $2.2 million an hour. But the wealthiest man in Brazil is only the eighth richest in the world—and top ten isn't good enough. Batista has openly stated that he plans to be number one before his sixtieth birthday, in 2016.

# O CRUZEIRO

DAVID NASSER en

O PADROEIRO DOS TA

# M
## MAGAZINES

Published from 1928 to 1975, *O Cruzeiro* was the most important Brazilian magazine of the twentieth century, and an influence on other popular publications like *Manchete*. Its early mix of photojournalism, sports, celebrity, fashion, cinema, and politics seems visionary today.

# B

## BOSSA NOVA

Bossa nova literally means "new trend," a reference to the smooth fusion of jazz and samba that developed in the 1950s in the upscale beach neighborhoods of Rio de Janeiro. As bossa nova's appeal grew internationally, singers like Dusty Springfield and Frank Sinatra recorded their own interpretations.

# CURITIBA

Although its flag motto is "Order and Progress," Brazil is seldom associated with rigor. The city of Curitiba, however, is one of the greenest in the world and a model of successful urban planning. Its public transport system, with buses running in their own lanes and using elevated stops with disabled access, has been adopted in countries ranging from Colombia to Malaysia.

# H

## HERCHCOVITCH, ALEXANDRE

The cool kid of Brazilian fashion, Alexandre Herchcovitch has incorporated skulls, Walt Disney characters, gigantic sequins, religious iconography, and fabrics that change color with the sun into his designs. Still, his clothes always maintain a sense of utilitarian ease.

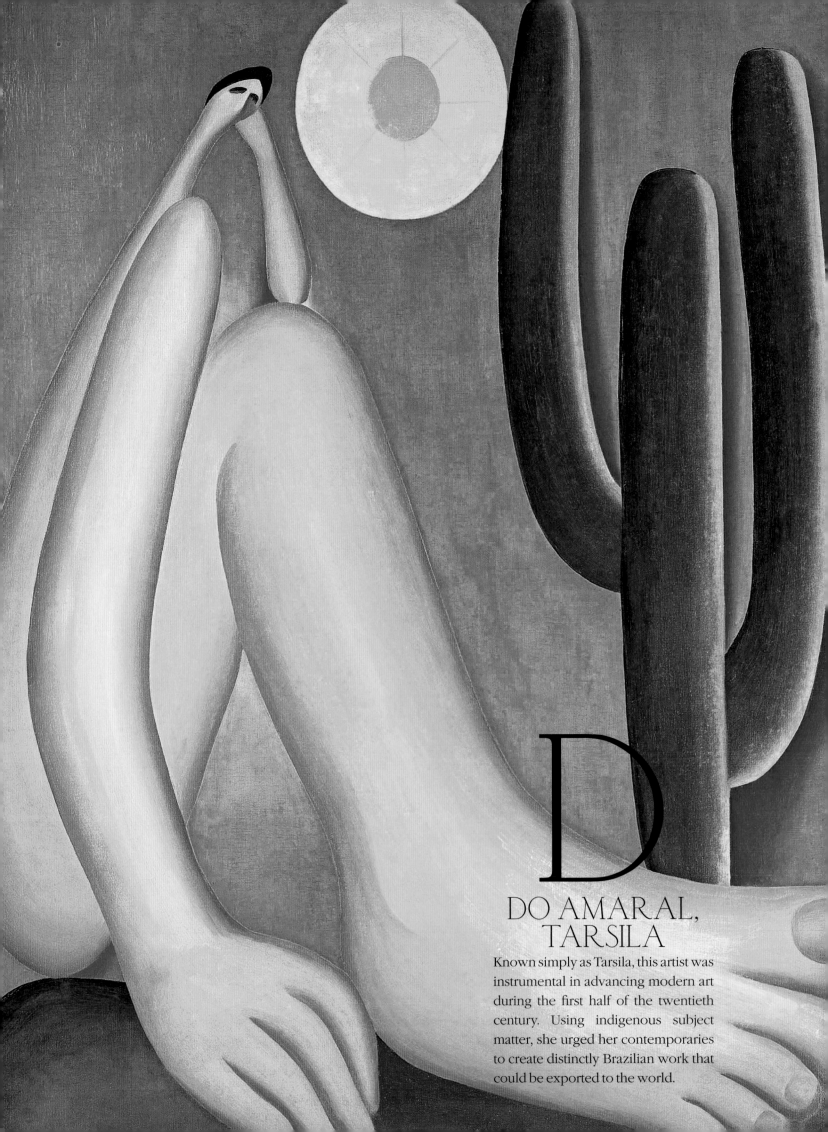

# D

## DO AMARAL, TARSILA

Known simply as Tarsila, this artist was instrumental in advancing modern art during the first half of the twentieth century. Using indigenous subject matter, she urged her contemporaries to create distinctly Brazilian work that could be exported to the world.

## OVO

An ovo is, quite simply, an egg. Cooked in boiling water with food coloring and sold in corner shops, the gaudy-hued snack is probably the most popular street food in Brazil.

# B

## BO BARDI, LINA

Modernist architect Lina Bo Bardi, who died in 1992, is best known for her Glass House in São Paulo's Morumbi neighborhood, as well as for the SESC Pompeia (pictured), a converted factory building that now contains theaters, galleries, restaurants, and a swimming pool.

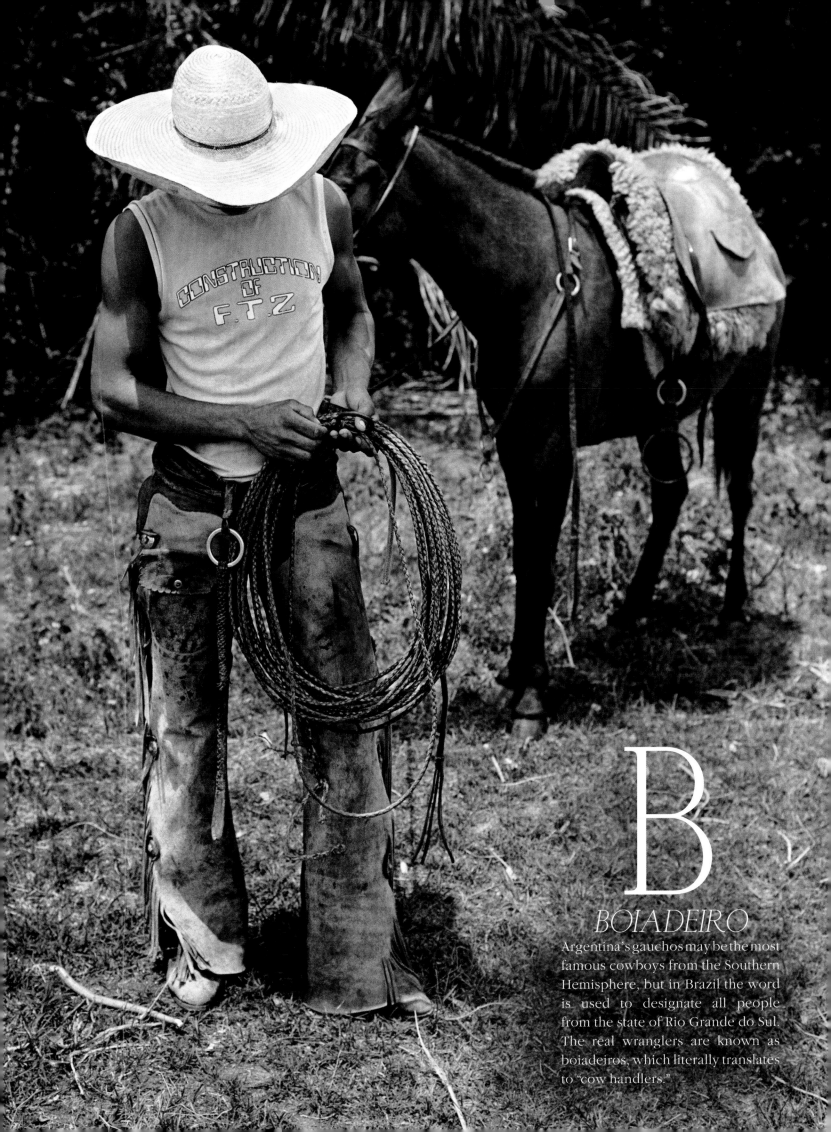

# B

## BOIADEIRO

Argentina's gauchos may be the most famous cowboys from the Southern Hemisphere, but in Brazil the word is used to designate all people from the state of Rio Grande do Sul. The real wranglers are known as boiadeiros, which literally translates to "cow handlers."

# OS GÊMEOS

Identical twins Otavio and Gustavo Pandolfo are Brazil's most famous street artists. Their work, which has been shown in museums and galleries all over the world, includes graffiti tags, trippy sculptures, and enormous murals with themes including hip-hop culture (they started out as break-dancers) and traditional folklore.

# P

## PIXAÇÃO

This form of graffiti, typical of São Paulo, is inspired by everything from political slogans to heavy-metal logos, and doesn't seek art-world recognition. The *pixadores,* or taggers, come from the city's poorest neighborhoods and are reviled by the police; their willingness to risk their lives scaling buildings in order to simply leave a mark suggests that they would rather be hated than ignored.

# F
## FERNANDO DE NORONHA

This volcanic island located two hundred miles off Brazil's north-eastern coast is a UNESCO World Heritage Site, and seventy percent of its territory is a protected Marine National Park. Tourism to Fernando de Noronha is strictly regulated, which is why more and more celebrities are hiding out there.

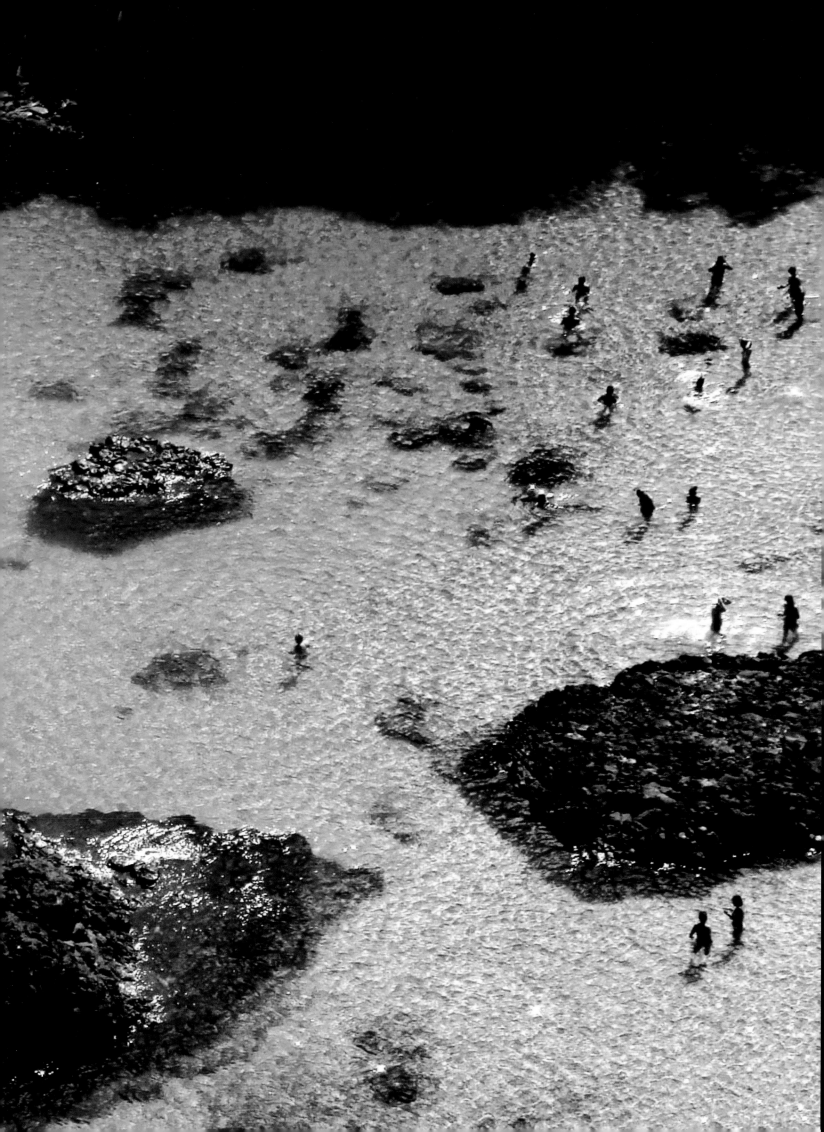

# B
## BLU AND JEWEL

Brazil's latest superstars are two macaws called Blu and Jewel. In the animated film *Rio,* the avian couple is busy fending off exotic-bird smugglers, but they still manage to get lost in the Amazon, visit a samba club, and check out Rio's sights, including the famous statue of Christ the Redeemer.

Se um dia eu voltar
à minha terra,
quero cantar
canções de alegria,
quero rever o meu
lar e os amigos...
quero te abraçar,
sentir o teu calor,
tão não digo!
Saudade, Saudade...
da minha terra,
das minhas flores...
Saudade, Saudade...
da minha terra,
das minhas flores...

# S

## SAUDADE

To try and explain what saudade means, Brazilians usually mention nostalgia, homesickness, and longing. It's no wonder the word appears in so many songs, including this one by Patrick Dimon:

If one day I return to my country
I want to sing songs of joy
I want to see my home and friends again
I want to hold you and feel your warmth
You can't imagine how much!
Saudade, saudade... of my country, of my flowers...
Saudade, saudade... of my country, of my flowers...

# INDEX

# ACKNOWLEDGMENTS

Special thanks to Paulo Borges, Nizan Guanaes and Donata Meirelles, Mônica Mendes and everyone at Mônica Mendes Communications, Graziela Peres, Mario Canivello, Robert Forrest, Adriana Bechara, and all my friends who helped with comments and suggestions.

*Armand Limnander*

The publisher would like to give special thanks to Nelson Alvarenga, Alessandro Horta, Gilberto Sayão, Bruno Medeiros, and Arnaldo Faissol at InBrands; Paulo Borges, Graça Cabral, Fabienne Muzy, Augusto Mariotti, Graziela Peres, Paulo Martinez, Mauro Braga, and Camila Silva at Luminosidade; Vik Muniz, Sonia Braga, Francisco Costa, Pelé, Milton Nascimento, Bethy Lagardère, Alice de Jenlis, Celso Grellet, Lillian Holtzclaw, Mônica Mendes, Graciela Lumi, Carol de Lara, Nuno Garcia, Sonia Quintella, Pedro Bonacina, Bob Wolfenson, Jeffrey Milstein, Gabriel Rinaldi, Daryan Dornelles, Thales Leite, Claus Lehmann, Renata Mein, Roberto Wagner, Vicente de Paulo, Sergio Menezes, Antonio Guerreiro, Pedro Kok, Matthieu Salvaing, Pete Turner, Christian Cravo, Andrea Dellal, Evelyn Becker, Jum Nakao, Fernando Gabeira, Yamê Reis, Alex Bueno de Moraes and Fernanda Martins at 1500 Gallery, Clare Molloy and Nick Koenigsknecht at Peres Projects, Eli Sudbrack and Christophe Hamaide Pierson, Jesus Perez and José Moscardi, Mariana Waldow at São Paulo Museum of Art (MASP), Marina Giustino at Instituto Zuzu Angel, Fernanda Valente at BPCM, Meg Malloy at Sikkema Jenkins Co., Ariane Pereira de Figueiredo at Projeto Hélio Oiticica, Bethanie Brady and Jennifer Mora at Lehmann Maupin, Guadalupe Requena and Cintia Mezza at Museo de Arte Latinoamericano de Buenos Aires (MALBA), Ana Lenice at Projeto Leonilson, Fabio Settimi, Léia Pereira, Joaquim Marçal F. de Andrade, Michelle Lederer at Calvin Klein, Tarsila do Amaral, Letícia Sales, Amauri Aguiar at Espasso, Tiago Cruz at Minotauro Sports, Heloisa Maia at Osklen, Ania Ostaszewski and Jennifer Wexler at Artisan House, Ana Paula Amorim at *Jornal do Brasil,* Dudi Machado, Catrina Kowarick, Tatiana Rosato and Dominic Ladet at Fasano Hotels, Jennifer Aborn at Redbull, Karen L. Preston at The Leading Hotels of the World, Ltd., Bianca Barros, Raquel Jorge, Erica Benincasa, Christian Franz Tragni, Christina Bhan, Francisco Freitas, Marcel Arêde, Mario Canivello, Daniel Sehn, Carlos Serrao, James Yang at Corbis, Suzanne Speich, Michael Shulman at Magnum, Justin Rose at Trunk Archive, Alison Rigney and Jeff Wendt at Everett Collection, Leigh Montville and Aaron Siegel at Condé Nast, Patrick Demarchelier Studio, Andrea Fisher at ARS, Nathalie Chalom at Content xp, Cristina Zappa at Instituto Moreira Salles, Bruno Pouchin at Roger-Viollet, Mary Scholz at Getty Images, Silka Quintero at The Granger Collection, Oren B. Silverstein at Alamy, Carolyn McGoldrick at AP Images, Triona Crowley at Terrie Tanaka, and Daniela Guimarães at SambaPhoto.

# PHOTO CREDITS